Intelligent Guides

Napa Valley and Sonoma

April 2018 edition

Benjamin Lewin MW
Copyright © 2016, 2017, 2018 Benjamin Lewin
Vendange Press
www.vendangepress.com

Without limiting the rights under copyright reserved above, no part of this publication may be reproduced, stored in or introduced into a retrieval system, or transmitted, in any form or by any means (electronic, mechanical, photocopying, recording or otherwise) without the prior written permission of both the copyright owner and the above publisher of the book. All enquiries should be directed to contact@vendangepress.com.

Preface

This guide covers the North Coast of California. The focus is on Napa and Sonoma Valleys, but I also include two areas to the south of San Francisco: the Santa Cruz Mountains and Mount Harlan. The first part discusses the region, and explains the character and range of the wines. The second part profiles the producers. There are detailed profiles of the leading producers, showing how each winemaker interprets the local character, and mini-profiles of other important estates.

In the first part, I address the nature of the wines made today and ask how this has changed, how it's driven by tradition or competition, and how styles may evolve in the future. I show how the wines are related to the terroir and to the types of grape varieties that are grown, and I explain the classification system. For each region, I suggest reference wines that illustrate the character and variety of the area.

In the second part, there's no single definition for what constitutes a top producer. Leading producers range from those who are so prominent as to represent the common public face of an appellation to those who demonstrate an unexpected potential on a tiny scale. The producers profiled in the guide represent the best of both tradition and innovation in wine in the region. In each profile, I have tried to give a sense of the producer's aims for his wines, of the personality and philosophy behind them—to meet the person who makes the wine, as it were, as much as to review the wines themselves.

Each profile shows a sample label, a picture of the winery, and details of production, followed by a description of the producer and winemaker. Each producer is rated (from one to three stars). For each producer I suggest reference wines that are a good starting point for understanding the style. Most of the producers welcome visits, although some require appointments: details are in the profiles. Profiles are organized geographically, and each group of profiles is preceded by maps showing the locations of producers to help plan itineraries.

The guide is based on many visits to Napa and other regions of the North Coast over recent years. I owe an enormous debt to the many producers who cooperated in this venture by engaging in discussion and opening innumerable bottles for tasting. This guide would not have been possible without them.

Benjamin Lewin

Contents

The Importance of Napa	4
Varietals versus Blends	3
Fog in Napa Valley	5
Climate and Terroir	7
The Napa AVA and sub-AVAs	10
A Lack of Old Vines	17
The Move to Ripeness	18
The Rise of Cult Wines	20
Famous Vineyards	22
Mountain Vineyards	25
The Style of Napa	27
Carneros	28
Sonoma	29
Pinot Noir in Russian River Valley	31
Chardonnay in Napa and Sonoma	35
Cabernet Sauvignon in Sonoma	36
Old Vines Zinfandel	38
Santa Cruz Mountains	40
Limestone in Mount Harlan	43
Vintages	44
Visiting the Region	46
Profiles of Leading Estates	48
Estates in Napa	49
Estates in Sonoma	112
Estates in Carneros	146
Estates in Santa Cruz	150
Estates in Mount Harlan	155
Mini-Profiles of Important Estates	157
Index of Estates by Rating	171
Index of Organic and Biodynamic Estates	171
Index of Estates by Varietal Specialty	173
Index of Estates by Appellation	174
Index of Estates by Name	177

Tables

The Top Grape Varieties	*4*
Napa AVAs	*13*

Appellation Maps

The North Coast	*6*
Napa Valley	*11*
Napa Mountain AVAs	*16*
Sonoma	*30*
Russian River Valley	*34*

Producer Maps

Symbols for Producers	*48*
Napa Valley	*49*
St. Helena	*50*
Rutherford-Oakville	*50*
Sonoma	*112*
Carneros	*146*
Santa Cruz	*150*

The Importance of Napa

Napa Valley has been at the very heart of the rise of New World wines. Until the famous Judgment of Paris tasting in 1976, when Cabernet Sauvignon and Chardonnay from Napa Valley placed ahead of Bordeaux and Burgundy, there was very little interest in wines from outside Europe. The tasting changed the situation dramatically; Napa Valley, and in due course other places in the New World, were taken seriously, starting the trend to consider wines in terms of single grape varieties. Yet at the time, there were few inklings in Napa that their wines were about to play a major part on the world stage.

The news of the tasting came as a shock in Napa. The immediate effect was to sell out the wines that had won—the Chateau Montelena Chardonnay and Stag's Leap Cabernet. But the more important, longer term effect was to validate the concept of high-end wines from Napa. Bo Barrett of Chateau Montelena recollects that up to then, it had been an uphill battle to get the wines into distribution on the East Coast. "The practical consequence was that distributors would take the wines," he says. The effect on style was to reinforce the view that Napa should compete with Bordeaux. "The Paris tasting had the effect that if we won there, we must be as good, and we should make wine more like Bordeaux," says Fred Schrader.

Attempts to produce wine in California go back for more than a century. Napa Valley was a mixture of vineyards and prune orchards at the start of the twentieth century. Wine labeled as "Claret" was more than half of production, and Zinfandel accounted for another third. White wine, in the form of "Riesling" was less than 10%. Many of today's vineyards were planted in place of prune orchards.

Attempts to produce wine in California go back for more than a century. Napa Valley was a mixture of vineyards and prune orchards at the start of the twentieth century. Prunes were more important than grapes; in fact, many of today's vineyards were planted in place of prune orchards.

Before Prohibition, wine labeled as "Claret" was more than half of production. White wine, in the form of "Riesling" was less than 10%. At the start of Prohibition in 1920, California had 100,000 acres of vineyards and was producing about 20 million cases of wine annually. Production of dry table wine was a bit greater than production of fortified (sweet) wine. At the end of Prohibition, Zinfandel, Alicante, and Carignan were two-thirds of plantings in California. White varieties had disappeared. The trend towards mass production varieties continued for the next half century.

After the adjustment to home winemaking during Prohibition, popular taste favored sweet wines, and California adjusted to the new market, in which fortified wines outsold dry wines by three to one. It was to take 40

Napa Valley is now a monoculture of vines all the way across the valley floor.

years to reverse the trend. A huge proportion of wine was sold as an alternative to spirits at the very low end, and became known as the "Skid Row Trade."

When the move to quality started in the 1970s, bulk production varieties accounted for more than 80% of all production. In whites, Colombard (not a variety usually associated with quality) was the major variety with 40% of plantings. Today, Bordeaux varieties account for 80% of black plantings, and Chardonnay accounts for almost 70% of white plantings.

Some date the modern era in Napa from 1966, when Robert Mondavi opened his winery, the first new winery to be built in Napa since Prohibition. New wineries have been the driving force in Napa's revival: three quarters of Napa's current 400 wineries have been established since 1966, and it's a striking measure of change that you can count on the fingers of one hand the number of producers profiled in this guide who even existed in 1970.

Napa Valley likes to present an artisanal impression. "95% of the wineries are family-owned," says the Napa Valley Vintners Association. This is somewhat misleading as half of the vineyard land is distributed among several hundred owners, but the other half is owned by fewer than 25 individuals or corporations. The largest owners have hundreds of acres; the smallest has only a couple. The median vineyard holding is about 85 acres.

The increasing price of land pushes a trend towards concentration as the owners of the first wave of expansion from the 1970s-1980s come up

Napa Valley is north of San Pablo Bay, and about hour from San Francisco.

to retirement: some estates pass to the next generation, but others sell to a large corporation. This is balanced by the creation of new wineries by enthusiasts, but the rising price of land, and increasing restrictions on winery construction, with limits on how much wine can be produced and how many visitors are allowed each day, makes this more difficult. The high cost of entry now requires significant resources, leaving the artisan vintner squeezed between conglomerates and lifestyle wineries.

For small estates, custom crush wineries sometimes offer an easier option than constructing a winery. Wheeler Farms is an up-market custom crush facility on Zinfandel Lane in St. Helena. In the nineteenth century, Wheeler Farms stretched over 2,000 acres and included a winery. Perhaps it's a sign of the times that after they sold Araujo Estate, Bart and Daphne Araujo bought a 12 acre parcel of Wheeler Farms which came with a winery permit, and constructed a custom-crush winery and hospitality building in 2015.

Varietals versus Blends

Today Napa Valley is closely associated with Cabernet Sauvignon, but Cabernet Sauvignon production was insignificant until the 1970s. Asked whether Cabernet Sauvignon was the obvious variety of choice when Joseph Phelps was established in 1973, Bill Phelps says, "Hardly. The first three years Riesling was the main variety. It wasn't clear Cabernet would be the future until the late seventies. At the start we planted Riesling, Pinot

> ## The Top Grape Varieties in Capsule
>
> *Cabernet Sauvignon* is the top black variety. The great variety of Bordeaux, in California it is often vinified as a varietal wine, but is sometimes blended with Merlot and other Bordeaux varieties. This gives the most powerful and structured wine of Napa; it is only a fraction leaner in Sonoma.
>
> *Pinot Noir* is the second most important variety in Sonoma, especially in Russian River Valley. It's also important in Carneros. The wines are richer and more powerful than those of Burgundy.
>
> *Zinfandel* is California's own black variety, although it is the same as Primitivo of southern Italy and Crljenak of Croatia. The wines are rich, fruity, and alcoholic. They are most common in Sonoma, especially Dry Creek Valley.
>
> *Chardonnay* is the leading white variety. The old style was rich and powerful, often vinified with a lot of new oak to give a buttery impression with vanillin overtones. Today there's a move towards a leaner style, more citrus-driven, in which malolactic fermentation is blocked to keep higher acidity.
>
> *Sauvignon Blanc* is grown in both Napa and Sonoma, often vinified and aged in oak in the Fumé Blanc style, so that it's more rich than herbaceous.

Noir, and Cabernet Sauvignon. During the 1980s we realized we couldn't do every variety and we focused on Cabernet Sauvignon."

As it became clear that Cabernet Sauvignon should be the black grape of choice, what were the producers' stylistic aims? When you decided on Cabernet, were you trying to compete with Bordeaux, I asked Bill Phelps? "Absolutely. The model was the first vintage of Insignia in 1974. Joe made it like a Bordeaux and really wanted it to be a blend." Have objectives changed since the first vintage? "Our style has changed. This was a decision. As Napa came into its own, we realized what was in the material and we could rely on the vineyards. In the 1970s, things were driven by winemaking, now they are more driven by what happens in the vineyards. There's still a strong affinity with Bordeaux, but now we have established our own identity."

Once Cabernet Sauvignon was established as the principal grape, if it was blended with other varieties in Napa, they were the usual suspects: Merlot, Cabernet Franc, and Petit Verdot. A split developed between those who believe that pure Cabernet Sauvignon gives the best results and those who believe that blending produces more complex wines, and this continues to the present.

Fog rolls into Napa Valley from the Pacific most mornings, and disperses around midday.

Wines labeled as Cabernet Sauvignon are allowed to include 15% of other varieties in most New World countries, and up to 25% in the United States. A large proportion of wines labeled as Cabernet Sauvi-gnon in Napa in fact are just over the 75% limit, so it would be a fine line to distinguish them from blends dominated by Cabernet Sauvignon.

Varietal-labeled Cabernet Sauvignon is Napa's main challenge to Bordeaux. The main alternative consists of Bordeaux blends with less than three quarters Cabernet Sauvignon, and most often these are described as Proprietary Reds. There is a category called Meritage, introduced in 1988 to describe wines based on a Bordeaux blend, but it never really impacted the mainstream, and has mostly disappeared.

Chardonnay has taken over as Napa's main white representative, and Sauvignon Blanc has become firmly established in second place. Both tend to show rich styles, but this is most evident for Sauvignon Blanc, especially when it is vinified in the Fumé Blanc style pioneered by Robert Mondavi, using barrel fermentation in oak (sometimes new oak, at that). Both Chardonnay and Sauvignon Blanc are usually vinified to make single varietal wines.

Fog in Napa Valley

Napa Valley itself is really quite a confined area. About 30 miles long and generally less than a mile wide, it nestles between the Mayacamas mountains to the west (separating Napa from Sonoma) and the Vaca mountains to the east. Looking across the valley, a difference is immediately apparent between the Mayacamas Mountains, which are covered in vegetation, and the Vaca Mountains, which have a distinctly scrubby appearance. Weather comes from the Pacific, and the east is drier than the west, because rainfall gets blocked by the Mayacamas Mountains.

The Mayacamas Mountains to the west are covered in evergreens.

Napa Valley has an abundance of that surprising key feature for wine production in California: fog. This is not usually welcome in wine-producing regions, but the climate in California would normally be too warm for fine wine production, and is rescued only by the regularity of the cooling fog. Almost all the top regions for wine production are in valleys that are cooled by fog rolling in from the Pacific Ocean. (The exceptions are vineyards at high enough elevations that cooling comes from the altitude.) Morning fog is fairly reliable in Napa, usually clearing around midday.

Because a high pressure system settles over the California coast each summer, the growing season tends to be warm and dry. Except for the absence of rain in the summer, the climate is perfect for agriculture. Irrigation fills the gap. Although most vineyards in Napa are irrigated, there is a slowly growing movement towards dry farming (meaning no irrigation). According to Christian Moueix, when he came from Petrus to establish Dominus: "I was determined to have dry farming (apart from the very young vines)... Dry farming encourages deep roots and is key for expressing terroir. I have not had the success I had hoped for to convince my friends to give up irrigation, they say the vines will die. No, they come from the Caucasus and can withstand anything. Unirrigated vines will naturally find their equilibrium and won't need to be picked as late as irrigated vines. Irrigation is one of the reasons you get these crazy alcohol levels in Napa."

The climate in Napa Valley escapes the European rule that temperatures become warmer going south; the northern end is decidedly warmer than

The hills to the east are dry and scrubby.

the southern end, because the more open southern end gets cooling breezes from San Pablo bay, whereas the narrow northern end is effectively closed. At the very southern end, Napa itself is close in temperature to Bordeaux; but Calistoga at the far north is more like the south of France, and it becomes too hot to grow Cabernet Sauvignon on the valley floor.

The hot, dry nature of the climate was brought home forcefully with the wildfires that raged in northern California in 2017. Few vineyards in Napa or Sonoma were directly damaged, but there were issues with possible smoke taint, as it's very difficult to remove from grapes that have been exposed. Producers who harvested before the fires were less at risk.

The collision between the three tectonic plates that created the valley some 150 million years ago left detritus of a great variety of soil types, with more than 40 different soil series classified in Napa. A major factor is the consistent difference between the warmer, and more fertile, valley floor, and the cooler terrain of the slopes to the west and the east. And moving from south to north, the soil changes from sediments deposited by past oceans to a more volcanic terrain, which also is prevalent on the mountains.

Climate and Terroir

Definition of individual regions, or more specifically identification of locations where particular varieties grow best, developed slowly after the growth of the 1960s. The spur for the realization that not all sites in Napa Valley were created equal was the definition by University of California

Wildfires came close to vineyards in Napa and Sonoma at the end of the season in 2017

professors Albert Winkler and Maynard Amerine in the 1940s of heat zones in Napa Valley. Classifying California into five zones according to average temperatures during the growing season, they recommended suitable grape varieties for each region. Among the varieties recommended for the cooler, southern part of the valley were Cabernet Sauvignon and Chardonnay, but it was not until the 1960s that growers paid much attention.

With the extension of grape growing from the valley floor (where it resumed after Prohibition) to the mountain slopes (planted after the revival of the seventies), there is considerable variation not only of terroir but also of climate. In fact, the most important determinant of climate may be elevation, rather than position along the valley. The original definition of heat zones mapped Napa into three zones, with the Carneros region at the southern end the coolest in zone 1, Napa itself in zone 2, but Oakville and St. Helena in warmer zone 3. More recent data confirm a gradual increase in average growing season temperatures going up the valley, but put the whole valley floor into zone 4, with conditions becoming significantly cooler moving up in elevation into the mountains on either side.

To the casual tourist—of whom there are more than five million annually—driving up Route 29 on the western side, or back down the Silverado trail on the eastern side, Napa Valley might appear quite homogeneous, a veritable sea of vines stretching across the valley between the mountains on either side. The land appears flat until close to the mountains. Taking any cross street between the two highways, you travel exclusively through vineyards. The Napa river in the center of the valley seems unimportant. The impression of dense plantation is true for the center of the valley, where three quarters of the land is planted with vines, but this apparent consistency is somewhat deceptive.

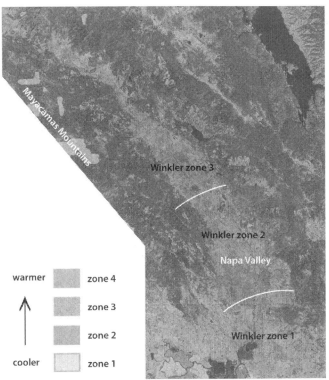

Climate mapping by Winkler originally divided the valley into three zones, becoming increasingly warmer going from south to north. More recent data suggest the main difference is between the valley floor and the slopes and mountains on either side.

The heart of the valley is characterized by alluvial fans, formed by streams that flowed out of the mountains. When a stream opens out on to a valley floor, it deposits sediment as it flows. Over time, the sediment causes the watercourse to shift sideways, creating a fan-like area of sediment, stretching from the slopes to the valley floor. Alluvial fans run continuously along the west side of the valley; the series is more broken up along the east side. Known locally as "benches," the most famous are the Oakville Bench and the Rutherford Bench, where production of fine wine started in the nineteenth century. (Valley floor tends to be used in two senses in Napa. Generally used as generic description to distinguish terrain between the mountain ranges as opposed to the steep slopes, it is not pejorative. Sometimes it is used more disparagingly to distinguish fertile soils from the alluvial fans.) Sediments become finer, and the soils that form on them become richer, as an alluvial fan widens out. Beyond the fan, soils on a valley floor can be too rich for producing fine wine.

"Terroir isn't everywhere. In fact, terroir is in very few places. I have five wines and one is a terroir wine," says Doug Shafer of Shafer Vineyards. "Hillside Select is a special place; it's planted with one hundred percent Cabernet Sauvignon, but it could be Merlot or Cabernet Franc and the special quality of the fruit would still come through." Doug feels that hillsides make better wine than flat lands, but that the gap has narrowed. "Originally we didn't have the tools to make wines from the valley floor. Changes in viticulture mean now you can make wine from the valley floor that is nearly as good as the hillside. You have to work harder; we used denser planting and canopy management to reduce yields. This was not possible ten years ago."

The Napa AVA and sub-AVAs

Well before any regulations were introduced, Napa Valley became an imprimatur of quality on the label. Following the precedent of the French system of appellation contrôlée, the AVA (American Viticultural Area) system was introduced in 1976. This defines a pyramid of wine-producing regions. A broad Napa Valley AVA covers the whole region: as the result of a highly political process, the boundaries go well beyond the valley itself and were drawn to include all vineyards regarding themselves as producing Napa Valley grapes. Covering a total area of 90,000 ha, which represents about half of Napa County, the AVA has about 18,500 ha of vineyards. Given the variation between the south and north, and between the valley floor and the mountains, this implies a certain lack of coherence.

AVAs are defined at the instigation of producers in a region, and there are presently fifteen smaller AVAs within the all-encompassing Napa Valley designation. They extend from appellations defining the central valley to mountainous slopes on either side. (Producers often use the term appellation rather than AVA, and will talk about their appellation or sub-appellation wines.) The sub-AVAs tend to have more integrity, and often indicate higher quality wines. About 40% of the vineyards are in the old areas, stretching from Yountville through St. Helena, at the heart of the valley.

Are there really discernible differences between AVAs in the valley? The answer is yes and no. There may be a core to each sub-AVA, but unfortunately the same sorts of political considerations came into play when defining the sub-AVAs that had much reduced the coherence of Napa Valley. The original proposal for the Stags Leap District, for example, expanded to the west, south, and north as producers on the edges clamored to be let in.

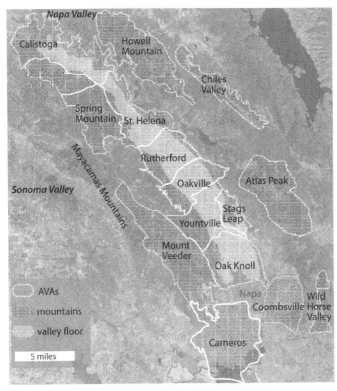

Napa Valley has several smaller AVAs within it. AVAs on the west and eastern sides are mountainous, but those in the center extend across both slopes and valley floor. (Carneros connects Napa and Sonoma valleys.)

The boundaries of the AVAs don't always make it easy to tell whether a particular wine has come from a valley or mountain. The AVAs in the valley often extend up the slopes of the mountains on either side. Pritchard Hill is well known for mountain Cabernets from the vineyards of Bryant, Chappellet, and Colgin, at elevations ranging from 120-330 m—but is included as part of the St. Helena AVA!

The most famous appellations of the valley proper have the most distinct reputations. The supposed characteristic of Rutherford is a dusty note in the wines. Whether Rutherford Dust is real or is a marketing ploy has long been debated. "The tannins of wines from Rutherford give the sensation you get by running your hand backwards along velvet," was an imaginative description by one producer. I do find a similar quality to the tannins in the wines of several producers. I would not describe it as dusty, more as a sort of distinctive tannic grip. But there are other producers whose wines typically have more massive or tighter tannins. I would be

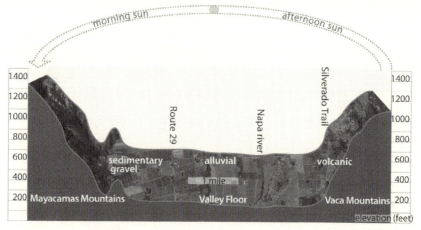

A cross section of the valley through the Oakville AVA shows variety of soil types and exposures to the sun.

prepared to concede a commonality in which firm tannins give the wines a quality I might be inclined to call Rutherford Grip, but more to the point, I find the wines of Rutherford always to have a slight aromatic lift that I do not find elsewhere.

In Oakville, the more common pattern is a quality of taut black fruits supported by fine-grained tannins that reinforce an impression of elegance. "Oakville is about expressing big berry fruits, a rich character with black olives, and more open tannins," says Mark de Vere of Mondavi. Some wines display a much softer style, with more overt, opulent black fruit aromatics extending from blackcurrants to cassis, and you might argue that they have deserted the communal specificity by going for more approachability in their vinification, but otherwise it is fair to say that Oakville is usually more powerful than Rutherford.

The problem with the AVAs in the heart of valley—Oakville, Rutherford, St. Helena—is that their reputation has been defined by the vineyards on the western side, running towards the slopes of the Mayacamas Mountains (basically by the classic region of the Oakville-Rutherford bench). While these may have consistent characters, the case for coherence is undercut by the extension of the AVAs right across the valley (and sometimes beyond it). Soils change from sedimentary gravel at the west to alluvial in the valley floor and to volcanic at the east. Exposure changes from the cooler morning sun of the western side to the hotter afternoon sun of the eastern side. What is valid along route 29 may very well not apply to the Silverado Trail.

Napa AVAs in Capsule

Valley AVAs

Calistoga is the far north and narrowest point of the valley. Chateau Montelena has a historic reputation, Eisele Vineyard has special terroir.

St. Helena extends around the town of St. Helena but stretches to the slopes of Spring Mountain to the west and to Pritchard Hill at the east. Vineyards run all the way from Spring Mountain to the west to Pritchard Hill to the east.

Rutherford is the heart of the valley with the top vineyards on the Rutherford Bench., making wines that are among the most elegant from the valley proper. Inglenook is the famous old name.

Oakville shares with Rutherford the core of the valley but is perhaps a little more powerful. Robert Mondavi is in the valley, Harlan is off to the west, and Screaming Eagle is on the Silverado Trail.

Stags Leap is one of the smaller AVAs with vineyards clustered around the Silverado Trail and is known for the velvety, lush quality of its tannins. Shafer Vineyards is the standard bearer today.

Yountville has never established any great reputation in its own name, but has the classic character of the valley proper. Dominus is its most famous vineyard.

Oak Knoll is just a touch cooler than the appellations in the heart of the valley.

Coombsville is a relatively new AVA for the area south of the town of Napa, and is the coolest area in the valley; producers are focusing on Chardonnay.

Mountain AVAs

Spring Mountain was one of the first mountain areas to be planted, notably by Diamond Creek, which has stayed true to its character since the beginning.

Mount Veeder was an early mountain region, characterized by Mayacamas Vineyards. Wines tend to be classically restrained.

Howell Mountain is restricted to vineyards above the fog line. Soils are low in fertility, vines can be stressed, wines can be taut. Dunn Vineyards is the epitome of the old style.

Chiles Valley is obscure and very few wines are labeled with the AVA.

Atlas Peak is rugged territory, with vineyards along the two roads running on either side of the mountain. Tannins can be aggressive. Kongsgaard is its most famous winery.

Wild Horse Valley is really off the beaten track, well away from Napa Valley, and relatively obscure.

Bryant Vineyards is the Pritchard Hill area at an elevation of 130 m overlooking Lake Hennessey. It is within the St. Helena AVA.

"Cabernets in Stags Leap tend to have richer fruit, with a softer texture," says Doug Shafer, who was instrumental in establishing the AVA. Shafer's Hillside Select, one of the top wines of the AVA, which comes from the vineyard rising up behind the winery, epitomizes this quality, with a style of opulent fruits showing evident aromatics. Doug supports his case by recollecting that when Shafer showed its first 100% Cabernet Sauvignon, it was so approachable that people refused to believe it had no Merlot.

But in Stags Leap District generally, I get less impression of consistency today, with many wines that are forward and approachable, showing soft black fruits on the palate, supported by nuts and vanillin on the finish, and tannins noticeable only as a soft, furry presence in the background. These are nice enough for something to drink immediately, but I wonder how it represents Cabernet typicity to make wines that are so fruit-forward and lacking in tannic structure. Again it's a producer's choice, but it seems more common in Stags Leap.

There may be a typicity that distinguishes each AVA if you let it express itself. In any of these appellations, however, you can make soft, forward, fruity, wines with lots of nutty vanillin, using appropriate winemaking techniques to bump up the appeal. Let's at least say that unless you know the producers' styles, the name of the AVA has little predictive value.

The area of the Napa Valley AVA extends far beyond the obvious tourist trails. Well off to the east are Howell Mountain, Chiles Valley, and Atlas Peak. To the west are Diamond Mountain, Spring Mountain, and Mount Veeder. Driving up the twists and turns of the densely forested roads into the mountains is a completely different experience from meandering along

The heart of Napa Valley, between Napa and St. Helena, has a monoculture of vineyards, extending across the narrow valley, confined by the mountains on either side.

the center of the valley. Mountain vineyards are sparsely planted, occupying perhaps 5% of the total land, contrasted with the monoculture in the valley itself.

The big difference in Napa is really between mountains and valley: these have different climates and soils. With vineyards often above the fog line, the climate in the mountains is quite distinct from the valley itself, where fog is the dominant (and saving) influence. The playoff is that temperatures are reduced by the elevation, but increased by the lack of fog. There is often more diurnal variation. Mountain vineyards have primary soils with more mineral or volcanic character, compared with the more alluvial soils deposited by water flow in the valley. Couple the climatic changes with the differences in the soils, and you may well ask what connection exists between the mountain vineyards and those in the valley to justify both being labeled under the same Napa AVA.

There's a growing tendency to plant Cabernet Sauvignon on hillsides and mountains rather than on the valley floor, and today about 14% of the vineyards and 20% of the wineries are on the mountains (mountain vineyards tend to be smaller). There is quite a bit of talk in Napa about "mountain tannins." Grapes grown on the mountains tend to have higher, and sometimes more aggressive, tannins; getting the tannins ripe at higher altitudes may require a long hang time, with the incidental consequence of later harvests. The grapes protect themselves from the combination of more sunshine (especially higher ultraviolet radiation) and greater wind exposure by increasing their production of anthocyanins and tannins. All this contributes to a tighter structure, especially when the vineyards are above the fog line.

Vineyards in the mountains have significant elevation above those in the valley itself, and conditions are quite different.

The mountains are not all the same. On opposite sides of the valley, Mount Veeder and Howell Mountain give the most taut impression of a fine backbone to the fruits. Atlas Mountain tannins are quite fierce: you have to go to the greater fruit intensity of the single vineyard wines to balance them out. Spring Mountain tannins are less obvious, not so much aggressive as just flattening the fruits.

Unlike the European system, the statement of an AVA on the label applies only to geographical origin; there is no additional implication of quality, grape variety, or style. When the rules were being discussed in 1979, André Tchelistcheff was sarcastic about the construction of AVAs. "We are not solving the basic elements of appellation, we are not controlling the varietals, we are not controlling the maximum production; I mean we are just trying to fool the consumer that we have appellation of origin."

An AVA label only requires that 85% of the grapes come from the AVA: my view is that this is nowhere near good enough. Considering the premium you pay for Napa Valley, a wine labeled from Napa should have only grapes from Napa. As for vintage, the rules have finally been tightened to specify that wine from an AVA must have 95% of its grapes from the stated vintage. For grape variety, the rule is 75%; this is probably as good as we are going to get, since it started out as 51% when the first federal regulations were introduced in 1936, and was increased (against some opposition) to 75% in 1983. The 75% rule leaves a lot of wiggle room, far too much in my opinion. I would like to see all the rules replaced with a 95% lower limit!

Because the focus on Cabernet Sauvignon is recent, there are not many old vines in Napa Valley. These fifty-year-old vines in the Kronos vineyard are among the oldest.

A Lack of Old Vines

Napa's character as a young wine region was prolonged by the need to replant many of the vineyards in the nineties. One of the glories of old vineyards is the extra concentration produced in the wine as the vines age. There's no exact measure for what the French would call Vieilles Vignes, but after about twenty years, the yields drop. Perhaps because the lower yields are achieved naturally, the extra concentration seems to have a focus and intensity that is not produced by simply reducing yields by extreme pruning. You might expect the vineyards that were planted during the boom of the 1970s now to have venerable old vines. Unfortunately, a problem with phylloxera put paid to that.

Because of its European origins, Vitis vinifera has no resistance to phylloxera; it must be grafted on to resistant rootstocks from American species of Vitis. Early plantings in Napa used the St. George rootstock, a cultivar of Vitis riparia, which is highly resistant to phylloxera. Its disadvantage is that it can lead the vine to be too productive. New plantings during the 1960s and 1970s tended to use AxR1, a rootstock recommended by the Enology Department at the University of California, Davis for its reliability. AxR1 is a hybrid between Vitis vinifera and Vitis rupestris; like many hybrids with some vinifera parentage, it is not really very resistant to phylloxera. The university should have known better, because by the late 1980s, quite predictably, phylloxera was enthusiastically feeding on these rootstocks; unfortunately, by then about 75% of plantings in Napa and Sonoma were on AxR1.

The need to replant vineyards in the 1990s was not entirely a bad thing. "As growers were forced to replant by phylloxera, a lot of the unspoken issues—rootstocks, clones, spacing—became issues for discussion," says Anthony Bell, who had been horrified to find when he came to Beaulieu in 1979 from South Africa that Napa had made itself so vulnerable by planting on a single rootstock. "This was something all Europeans had been told you didn't do," he says.

Any vines more than, say, 60-years-old are likely to be Zinfandel. The only old Cabernet vines in Napa today are those planted on St. George before the phylloxera epidemic. Sometimes this was the result of calculation, sometimes it was luck, and sometimes *force majeure*. When Al Brounstein created Diamond Creek Vineyards in 1968, he was under pressure to plant AxR1, but he stuck to St George because it had a good record in the mountains. When Cathy Corison purchased her vineyard in Rutherford in the 1990s, the price was reduced because it was thought to be on AxR1—but in fact turned out to be on St. George, and at over forty years old, the vines today are some of the oldest in the valley. When Chateau Montelena planted vineyards in 1974, they tried to do the conventional thing and use AxR1, but it was in so much demand they couldn't get any, so they used St. George. "We were lucky rather than smart," Bo Barrett recalls happily. A side effect of the replacement of AxR1 since the nineties has been an increase in ripeness; the new rootstocks encourage lower yields and more rapid ripening.

Replanting as the result of the AxR1 debacle forced attention on the selection of the cultivar as well. Clones attract more attention in Napa Valley than perhaps anywhere else that focuses on Cabernet Sauvignon. Until the early nineties, there was little choice, but then the French ENTAV clones from Bordeaux became available as well as the so-called heritage clones that had been propagated from vines previously grown in California. The question about the move towards the ENTAV clones is whether material that was selected in a relatively cool period in Bordeaux will necessarily give the best results in Napa's warmer and drier climate.

The Move to Ripeness

Napa's view on the appropriate style for Cabernet Sauvignon has evolved. As Napa began its revival, the general view was that Bordeaux was about elegance, and California was about power. Initially Napa Valley set out to compete with Bordeaux, but by the 1990s came around to the view that the wine should be in a richer style more reflecting its warmer climate. This has been the basis of a continuing debate as to whether Cabernet Sauvignon (and for that matter wines based on other varieties) should reflect the character of the places where they originated in Europe, or should show a more "international" style reflecting the new places where they are made.

Fred Schrader, who has been associated with cult wines since the early nineties, thinks the change in style is an appropriate reflection of conditions in Napa. "In the mid eighties, people wanted to make wine just like Bordeaux. I was never part of that school, my attitude was why do we care? The climate and actually the seasons here are different. We have a hotter climate, with riper berries; we are more fruit forward. We should not try to emulate, we should try to make something that reflects who we are."

The style changed in the early nineties. "When I was running Beaulieu, by the late eighties, we were trying to change the style of our wines," says Anthony Bell. "By the mid nineties we were in our stride. Probably the period from 1990-1995 was when things changed." Anthony quotes a telling example of the change in style. "Today the reserve wines are made from grapes picked at the end of the season, but when I joined BV the Reserve was made from grapes picked first—because they came from the healthy vineyards that gave the best quality grapes."

The move to the riper, more "international" style was partly driven by critics who scored the wines highly—or perhaps more to the point, scored restrained wines poorly. Many people feel that influential critic Robert Parker had a major effect in driving the trend, especially the singling out of "100 point" wines that were almost always powerful and fruit-driven.

Attempts at a European aesthetic in Napa were criticized. There was a long-running difference of opinion between Mondavi and the *Wine Spectator* over style. The *Spectator's* lead critic on California, James Laube, commented in July 2001, "At a time when California's best winemakers are aiming for ripe, richer, more expressive wines, Mondavi appears headed in the opposite direction... [Winemaker] Tim Mondavi and I have different taste preferences... He has never concealed his distaste for big, ultra rich plush or tannic red wines. I know he can make rich, compelling wines, yet he prefers structured wines with elegance and finesse... the attempt to give his wines more nerve and backbone has come at the expense of body and texture... he's decided to turn his back on a climate ideally suited for producing ripe, dramatic wines, and rein in those qualities so that the wines show restraint rather than opulence."

Tim Mondavi replied, "I am concerned... that while global wine quality has improved tremendously, there appears to be a current trend toward aggressively over-ripe, high in alcohol, over-oaked wines that are designed to stand out at a huge tasting rather than fulfill the more appropriate purpose of enhancing a meal."

There you have the whole debate in a nutshell. It's hard to defy the rush to ripeness: the price is likely to be lack of critical acclaim. Over recent decades, the story of Cabernet Sauvignon in Napa has been the struggle to control its ripeness. The same is true of other varieties: over-ripeness is the main reason why Merlot has not been successful and why producers have backed away from Chardonnay.

The Rise of Cult Wines

The nature of the high end has changed since Napa started concentrating on Cabernet. In 1974, many of the top wines were "Reserves," coming from Beaulieu, Mondavi, or Louis Martini. "Reserve really didn't mean much, although the term was popular at the time. Benziger destroyed the use of the term by making a bulk wine. I always resented that. It was quite different from Estate but even that has been diluted now," says Richard Arrowood, one of the first winemakers to focus on single vineyard wines (in Sonoma).

Today the top wines tend to come from single vineyards, often enough carrying the name of the sub-AVA in which they are located. (However, worried about possible dilution of identity, Napa Valley vintners sponsored a law in 1990 that all wines attributed to any AVA within Napa should in addition mention Napa Valley.) Is the switch in emphasis from reserve bottlings to single vineyards a mark of a maturing wine region?

Although there is a definite move towards single vineyards, there are still some leading wines based on barrel selections. It may be true that single vineyards become more interesting at very small production levels, but blending produces more complexity at higher levels. "Separate vineyard wines from the mountains and valley would be like putting handcuffs on us. Not all lots turn out great every year and quality bounces around the valley like a ball. There's wide variation in sources from year to year. In a cool year, St Helena and Calistoga make the best lots, in a warm year it's Napa and the hillsides," says Chuck Wagner, explaining that Caymus Special Selection is usually a blend of one quarter from mountain sources and three quarters from the valley.

"A cult wine is a wine that you hear all about but never get to taste" is not a bad definition. There have always been wines recognized as hors de classe, of course, but the first growths of Bordeaux, and top Burgundies such as Domaine de la Romanée Conti, are available in the marketplace, even if very expensive. The cult wines of Napa are a more artificial phenomenon, often not for sale in general distribution and available only by an allocation to private customers for which there is a long waiting list. They are expensive: the situation is captured by a quote from a producer in 2006: "On several occasions we have had difficulty selling wines at $75, but as soon as we raise the price to $125 they sell out and get put on allocation."

At the start of the cult wine phenomenon, many small producers shared a tasting room at the Napa Wine Company in Oakville, indicated by the sign to Cult Wine Central

Reputation may depend either on the producer's name or the vineyard. Often enough the same consultants are involved: David Abreu, Heidi Barrett, Helen Turley, Philippe Melka, Michel Rolland, all known for managing vineyards for low yields, or winemaking for high extraction. Their names give instant credibility to new ventures to create cult wines.

Some producers set out from the start to produce only cult wines, using a combination of extreme methods of viticulture and vinification (not unlike the creation of garage wines in Bordeaux) to produce very intense wines. Screaming Eagle is often credited with starting the phenomenon with its inaugural 1992 vintage. Within three or four years, Araujo, Bryant, Colgin, and Harlan followed with the explicit intention of repeating the phenomenon. Now there are many more.

Some vineyards have acquired cult reputations, such as Beckstoffer's various plots in To-Kalon. Those producers who can afford to purchase the grapes produce small quantities of wine at high prices that often achieve cult status. Schrader was one of the first to start the bandwagon by producing a variety of very limited-production runs from different parts of the vineyard.

When the cult is a vineyard, production is necessarily limited, but in many cases the small production is more a matter of managed scarcity. Production is usually less than 10,000 bottles per year. There is a certain commonality of style to most cult wines: they are almost always dominated by Cabernet Sauvignon, sometimes monovarietal. In many cases, the general policy is "more is better," but it would be naïve to dismiss all cult wines as being monolithic monsters. I do find those that are blends to offer more flavor interest and to age better: Screaming Eagle and Harlan would be good examples.

Prompted partly by the wish to maintain quality (and exclusivity), and partly by difficulties with the economy, the trend to offer second wines accentuated in Napa after the recession of 2008. They have a variety of origins: for cult wines produced in small quantities, they usually come from declassified lots; at larger producers they may represent different sources of material.

Famous Vineyards

Some of the top sites in Napa Valley have long histories, with potential that was recognized more than a century ago. At the heart of the Oakville area is the To Kalon vineyard, a parcel of almost 100 ha originally purchased by Hamilton Crabb in 1868 (the name is Greek for "most beautiful"). Further purchases brought Crabb's total to more than 150 ha. Half of the land was planted with hundreds of grape varieties within a few years. Wine was produced under the name of To Kalon vineyards; the best known was "Crabb's Black Burgundy," which actually was made from the Italian Refosco grape. But Cabernet Sauvignon was also grown there in the 1880s.

After various vicissitudes, including changes of ownership, Prohibition, and destruction of the original winery, the vineyard fell into various hands. The major part of more than 100 ha eventually ended up with Robert Mondavi, whose new winery was positioned at the edge of the original To Kalon vineyard. A minor part of the original To Kalon estate was purchased by Beaulieu Vineyards in 1940, and became the heart of Beaulieu's Private Reserve, but was sold to Andy Beckstoffer in 1993. Beckstoffer sells grapes to a variety of producers, and some of Napa Valley's most expensive Cabernets come from this parcel. It's a measure of the reputation of the vineyard that its grapes from the best known parts sell for close to ten times the average price for Napa Valley Cabernet Sauvignon.

The last, smallest part of the original To Kalon vineyard is a parcel of 8 ha that Crabb himself donated to the University of California; this now forms their Oakville Experimental Station. (Probably the most expensive terroir for an experimental station anywhere in the world!)

The To Kalon vineyard occupies the top half of the Oakville Bench— the apex of the fan is more or less at the top of the vineyard. The terroir is a gravelly loam, forming a gradual slope (only just noticeable to the eye) from an elevation of about 75m at the base of the mountains to 50m at the highway. Of course, To Kalon is large for a high quality vineyard, roughly three times the size of the average Grand Cru Classé of the Médoc, so it has significant variation. "Up by the hills it's grand cru terroir, and the

Looking down the To Kalon vineyard from the apex of the alluvial fan, there's a slight gradient down to route 29. The scrubby hills beyond the Silverado trail are in the background.

wine goes into the Reserve, towards the middle it's premier cru level, and the wine goes into the Oakville Cabernet, down by route 29 it's village territory and the wine goes into a Napa bottling," says Mark de Vere at Mondavi.

Just above the To Kalon vineyard is Heitz's famous Martha's Vineyard. The Martha's Vineyard 1974 was the first wine from Napa that fooled me at a blind tasting into thinking it came from Bordeaux. I had to be shown the bottle to be convinced I had made a mistake. This hundred percent Cabernet Sauvignon comes from a 35 acre vineyard on the Oakville Bench, just above the To Kalon vineyard. The vineyard itself is not easy to find; there are no signs or directions—perhaps Heitz don't want it covered in day trippers.

The vineyard was owned by Tom and Martha May, and after a handshake deal, Joe Heitz started to produce wine from its crop in 1966. It was one of the first single vineyard wines of the modern era. The wine is often said to have a minty taste, and even the Heitz web site mentions the string of eucalyptus trees at the edge of the vineyards close to the base of the mountains, but Joe Heitz is reputed to have believed that the mintiness actually was a property of the vines (which are claimed to come from a proprietary clone producing unusually small berries). (But when Opus One acquired a block of the To Kalon vineyard on the other side of the trees, they did not like the minty taste in their wine, and cut down some of the trees.)

With some shade from the mountains close by, Martha's Vineyard is a little less sunny than some others; possibly this contributes to a slightly

The eucalyptus trees at the edge of Martha's Vineyard may have something to do with its famous minty aroma. The Opus One block of To Kalon is on the far side of the trees.

cooler climate impression and lower alcohol. "For more than two decades, Heitz Martha's Vineyard was the benchmark by which California Cabernets were judged," said Frank Prial of the New York Times in 2000. More recently it has of course followed the inevitable trend towards greater extraction and higher alcohol, but the wine remains relatively restrained for Napa. 1974 probably remains its greatest vintage.

Just across the road from Mondavi, Opus One was one of the first collaborations between Bordeaux and Napa. When Robert Mondavi and Baron Philippe de Rothschild announced the venture, it was seen as a validation of Napa as a winemaking region. Opus One is a Bordeaux Blend dominated by Cabernet Sauvignon (around 85%). An even clearer example of French influence on Napa is Dominus winery, located on the old Napanook vineyard, which was one of the first vineyards in Napa Valley, planted on the Oakville alluvial fan by George Yount in 1838. The vineyard was bought in 1943 by John Daniel, owner of Inglenook, and he kept it when he sold Inglenook in 1970.

Dominus was first produced as a partnership between Christian Moueix of Château Pétrus in Pomerol and John Daniel's daughter, and then in 1995 Christian became sole owner. The change in varietal constitution over the years is one sign of the adjustment from Bordeaux to Napa. "When Dominus started we had 21% Merlot; now it's only 0.2%. Cabernet Sauvignon has gone from 65% to 85%. The initial plantings were pre-

Viader Vineyards is on Howell Mountain (although outside the AVA) on a 32-degree slope overlooking Bell Canyon (a source of the drinking water supply for St. Helena).

judged from Bordeaux, that you could transpose percentages from Bordeaux to Napa and it would work," says winemaker Tod Mostero.

Mountain Vineyards

When Hamilton Crabb planted the To Kalon vineyard, it was just a matter of clearing the land and digging in the grapevines. Switching the use of the land to viticulture, especially as it becomes a monoculture, creates a certain change in the environment, but the terroir remains recognizably the same. This has not necessarily remained true as vineyard plantings have extended to mountains. When the first vineyards were carved out of mountain sites around Napa in the 1960s and 1970s, no one thought much of it (aside from questioning whether the sites were appropriate for the intended varieties).

By the 1980s, people began to object to terraforming. One trigger was the construction of Atlas Peak Vineyards. As described by the project manager, Dick Peterson, "There are D10 Cats up there. This is a moonscape, but we're ripping it. We'll put terraces in there...We'll fill that canyon with rocks the size of Volkswagens, then cover it up with some muck from the caves we're digging."

Mountain reconstructions became controversial. When Delia Viader constructed her vineyard on Howell Mountain, environmental damage to

Harlan Estate, which made one of the first "cult" wines in Napa, is on the mountain slopes at Oakville, looking out over Martha's Vineyard, To Kalon, and Napanook, lower in the valley.

Bell Canyon Reservoir below led to civil law suits and criminal charges. Today the growth of mountain vineyards has slowed dramatically. Given the much higher costs associated with creating and maintaining mountain vineyards, it's not surprising that they should include a concentration of high-end wineries; indeed, many of Napa's cult wines come from mountain sites.

Perhaps at the end of the day (environmental issues aside) the question is not whether a terroir is natural or artificial, but whether it is good for growing grapes. Or in the context of Cabernet Sauvignon, what's the difference in making wine from grapes grown on a mountain as opposed to in the valley? Indeed, it's curious that attempts in Napa to produce wines like Bordeaux should focus on mountain vineyards. Bordeaux, after all, is pretty flat, and the principal distinction between sites is whether they are gravel-based or clay-based. Christian Moueix thinks there is a problem. "In Napa the current obsession is with elevation and hillside sites. I think hillside vineyards are a big mistake. They need irrigation and anyway it's not a natural habitat for vines."

Bill Harlan at Harlan Estate (on the mountain above Oakville) and Al Brounstein at Diamond Creek Vineyards (on Diamond Mountain) were pioneers in believing that vineyards in the valley would not give the small berries that they needed for the highest quality Cabernet Sauvignon. "I wanted to create a first growth in California. All at once I started looking for a totally different type of land that would produce the best fruit, not necessarily look nice. Historically the best wine produced in America over a long period of time was the Rutherford Bench, but after studying soils I became convinced we wanted to be on the hillside with good drainage," says Bill Harlan. "Al felt that grapes from hillsides suffer more, and would give more intensity," Phil Ross at Diamond Creek recalls.

The Style of Napa

"Napa Valley is more a concept than a sense of place—it has become a brand and a style in itself," one producer said to me. "Napa Cabernet is the only New World wine ruler that's being used internationally—it wins price, volume, and scores. The reason it's the market winner is because the word *Napa* is a brand," says Leo McCloskey, of Enologix, a company that advises producers on how to increase the impact of their wines in the marketplace.

The question about Napa is to what extent there is uniformity of style, and how important are climate and land as opposed to winemaking? It's probably fair to say that winemaking with Cabernet Sauvignon is less variable than with some other varieties. The most significant factor affecting style is the choice of when to harvest, and certainly the trend towards achieving greater ripeness by later harvesting has played to Napa's general strengths: lots of sunshine and not much water. Insofar as there is a common style, it's an emphasis on ripe fruits that is encouraged by the climate.

Napa has come a long way from the era when the Wine Institute (an advocacy group representing producers) used the slogan, "Every year is a vintage year in California." That was behind the belief that persisted through the seventies that wine is made by winemaking. Site location and vineyard management were all but dismissed as relevant factors, and it was assumed that California's climate ensured perfect ripeness every year. "The predominant thinking at the time was that every variety would give good results if planted in a good place," Bill Phelps recalls. Matching terroir to varieties and taking account of climatic variation came later.

Today at top producers there is more concern to represent the terroir, and recognition that each vintage is different. Indeed, there's a certain disdain at the top Napa producers for technological advice from graduates of the Enology Department of the University of California, Davis. "Graduates from Davis know how to take care of chemicals and things," Fred Schrader says somewhat dismissively. Recollecting Napa's revival, Paul Roberts of Harlan Estate says, "There was the era of students from Davis who came here and said: 'That's how we make wine—going after the correct numbers.' This lasted into the eighties. Today there is more purity and less intervention; we measure numbers but we don't let it drive winemaking." That's the artisanal view.

Alcohol levels have gone up steadily in Napa. In 1975 they were not terribly different from Bordeaux, typically about 12.5% for Cabernet Sauvignon. They increased until peaking around 14.5% in 2004-2208, then declined, and went back up in 2012-2014. Christian Moueix is a bit sarcastic about this. "Remember, before vines arrived in the Napa Valley, there were prunes. The dominant flavor in Napa wines today is prune—it's natural. It's not an unpleasant taste but it's extreme."

Carneros

With increasing recognition that Napa Valley is really a relatively warm region, producers interested in Pinot Noir and Chardonnay have turned to cooler sites. Some Napa producers now make their Chardonnay from Coombsville, the coolest part of Napa Valley south of the town of Napa. Farther south, Carneros was the first area recognized as having potential for Pinot Noir. Today Pinot Noir and Chardonnay form the focus of the 9,000 acres of vineyards in Carneros. Some of the production goes for sparkling wine, but this has been cut back in recent years. Carneros shares the honors for Burgundian varieties,. and perhaps has been somewhat eclipsed, by Russian River Valley just to the north in Sonoma.

At the base of the valley that joins the Napa and Sonoma Valleys, Carneros is a curious area, rather depressed before viticulture was introduced, not to say a derelict dumping ground for trash. Viticulture did not make a great impact here until Francis Mahoney planted Pinot Noir at Carneros Creek Winery in 1972. Other vineyards followed through the 1980s, mostly owned by producers from Napa Valley.

The terroir is not the most obvious for Pinot Noir, since the soils are mostly clay, typically fairly shallow (about a meter deep), with poor drainage, but this is ameliorated by rather low rainfall. Going south towards San Pablo Bay, clay content increases in the soil and the clay turns from gray to black. The climate is dominated by cool breezes blowing from the expanse of San Pablo Bay; sometimes the "breezes" are strong winds.

Does wine from Carneros have a distinct character? If you directly compare Carneros Pinot with Russian River Pinot Noir made by the same producer, you see a consistent difference. Russian River tends to be more immediately generous, the first impression being the sumptuous quality of the fruits; Carneros tends to show its structure more clearly, in the form of more evident tannins.

Anne Moller Racke of Donum Estate captures the difference. "There is a Carneros typicity, it is more linear but has more layering [than Russian River] although the technical measurements of progress through the growing season are similar. Russian River has coolness from fog, Carneros from wind, which gives thicker skins and more linear tannins." (And if you go north of Sonoma, to Anderson Valley in Mendocino County, where some producers also have vineyards, you see a generally leaner style to the wines.)

Sonoma

"Napa is all about Cabernet Sauvignon and Bordeaux varieties, Sonoma is a jigsaw of varieties and is about diversity," says Mark Lingenfelder of Chalk Hill Winery. Sonoma County is about twice the area of Napa County, but has a comparable area of vineyards: reflecting their relative positions in the hierarchy of California wine regions, the crop is somewhat larger, but its value is somewhat less. Napa's historic concentration on Cabernet Sauvignon for reds and Chardonnay for whites has led to its being viewed as the leader for both, but in fact Sonoma produces three times as much Chardonnay as Napa and almost as much Cabernet Sauvignon. Cabernet is the most important black variety grown in Sonoma, but there is almost as much Pinot Noir. "In Napa, Cabernet is king, but in Sonoma it's more one of a variety of grapes," says winemaker Margo Van Staaveren at Chateau St. Jean.

The feeling in Sonoma is quite different from Napa. Sonoma Valley is much less confined than Napa Valley. The Coastal Range Mountains are well off to the west between Sonoma and the Pacific, and the Mayacamas Mountains are away to the east. Driving right through Sonoma, route 101 is a highway with the usual depressing industrial developments on either side once you enter the valley above Petaluma. This is quite a contrast with the chic wineries and tasting rooms along route 29 in Napa.

But when you get off the beaten track, there are numerous winding roads running through hillside slopes patterned with vineyards; wineries are indicated rather discretely. Several of the valleys come together at Healdsburg, a gentrified town just off the freeway. The average scale of production in Sonoma is smaller; vineyards are divided among 1,800 growers, compared with 600 vineyard owners in Napa.

Sonoma County is a relatively large area, extending from the coast to the Mayacamas Mountains separating it from Napa County. Labeled Sonoma County, a wine can come from anywhere in the area. Only a minor step up, Sonoma Coast is a vast coastal area without particularly distinguished terroir, although within it are some individual vineyards with good reputations. Coming to the regions of highest quality, it might be more appropriate to talk about the valleys of Sonoma in the plural, since in addition to the eponymous Sonoma Valley itself, there are several other valleys, each with its own characteristics.

Sonoma County has 15 AVAs (some contained within others). Only the major areas are shown here.

The AVA of Sonoma Valley is to the north of the town of Sonoma, centered on the Sonoma river. The other areas of interest are the valleys formed by rivers that drain into the Sonoma river (a contrast with Napa Valley, where the areas of interest are the mountain slopes on either side of the valley bottom). The best known valleys in Sonoma are the Russian River Valley (for Pinot Noir), Alexander Valley (for Cabernet Sauvignon), and Dry Creek Valley (for Zinfandel).

Closer to the breezes and fogs from the Pacific, Sonoma is on average cooler than Napa, with growing season temperatures in Santa Rosa, on the edge of the Russian River Valley, up to a degree less than Napa. This is why Pinot Noir can succeed in Sonoma while it is rarely successful in Napa. By the same measure, Cabernet Sauvignon might be expected to show more of a cool climate character. Microclimates are if anything more important in Sonoma than Napa, with wide variation in soils and temperatures. There's more Cabernet Sauvignon in the warmer valleys, Alexander, Dry Creek, and Sonoma, and very little in Russian River, which has a sharp focus on Pinot Noir.

Although there's a great diversity of soil types in Sonoma, possibly it's more to the point that terrains vary from valley floor, to rolling hills, to mountainous. Russian River Valley is the most consistent, with some vineyards on the flat land along the river, and the rest on low, gentle slopes. The most dramatic contrasts are to be found in Alexander and Sonoma Valleys, which vary from vineyards on relatively fertile flat soil in the center to vertiginous slopes up to several hundred meters of elevation on the mountains.

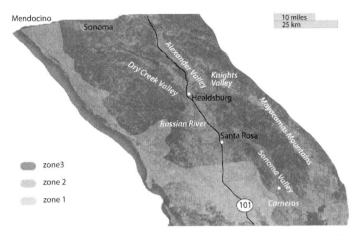

The climate becomes steadily warmer moving inland. Alexander Valley, Dry Creek Valley, and parts of Sonoma Valley are the warmest sites.

Dry Creek and Alexander Valleys run parallel to the north of Healdsburg. Closer to the coast, Dry Creek is a broad valley, cool at the southern end and warm at the northern end, growing a wide range of varietals from Pinot Noir at the south, to Cabernet in the middle, and Zinfandel in the north. It's by far best known for its Zinfandels, and indeed perhaps this is the one region in California where Zinfandel can be taken seriously as a grape that reflects terroir and produces ageworthy wines.

With that perverse reversal of the usual north-south, cool to warm, relationship, Alexander Valley, the most northern AVA of Sonoma, is where Cabernet Sauvignon does best. The Cabernets lack that extreme lushness found in Napa Valley and can offer a more restrained impression, as indeed also can the Zinfandels, especially those from around Geyserville, which rival those of Dry Creek Valley.

Pinot Noir in Russian River Valley

Pinot Noir has had a chequered history in California. Attempts to grow it for varietal production during the initial burst of enthusiasm for European varieties in the late nineteenth century were largely unsuccessful. In fact, wines labeled as "Burgundy" were as likely to be made from Zinfandel as from Pinot Noir. After the debacle of Prohibition, Pinot Noir was pioneered by Louis Martini in Carneros, but never achieved any penetration comparable to Cabernet Sauvignon. Part of the problem was the failure to define appropriate viticultural conditions for Pinot Noir, which was often planted next to Cabernet Sauvignon in sites that were simply too warm for it. And vinification was not adjusted for the variety. Josh Jensen, a Pinot Noir en-

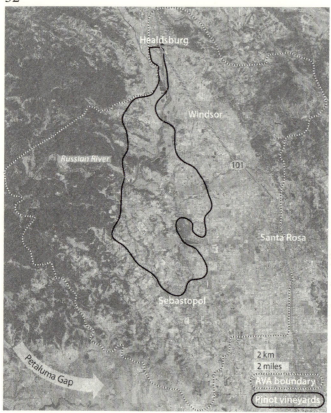

The Russian River AVA extends south of Healdsburg and includes most of Sonoma's Pinot Noir vineyards.

thusiast, comments that "most wineries had a standard red wine method" that was applied indiscriminately.

Attempts to produce quality Pinot Noir started in the 1970s, some of the pivotal moments being in 1973 when Joe Swan released his first Pinot Noir from Russian River, and Davis Bynum produced the first single vineyard Pinot Noir (from the Rochioli vineyard). More idiosyncratic in his choice of location, Josh Jensen planted the first vineyards for Calera Wine on Mount Harlan in 1975. But during the seventies and eighties, many wineries gave up attempts to produce Pinot Noir as part of a general belief that Pinot Noir belonged in Burgundy, not California. Looking back, Rod Berglund of Joseph Swan Vineyards comments that, "The oldest vines in the estate were planted in 1969. Anyone who planted Pinot Noir at that time was a visionary or a lunatic, and to say they were a visionary is revisionist history."

Russian River has gently rolling hills.

Pinot Noir is grown all over Sonoma, and bottlings range from Sonoma Coast AVA, meaning anywhere in the vast area, to single vineyard names. Because of geological history, there is a great variety of soil types; indeed, they are fond of saying locally that there are more soil types in Sonoma Valley than in the whole of France. The best known area is the Russian River Valley.

Running to the south of Healdsburg, Russian River Valley is Pinot Noir Central. The style is richer than Burgundy. "We don't make Burgundy and don't try to. We make Russian River Pinot Noir," says Bob Cabral, former winemaker of Williams-Selyem, whose single-vineyard Pinots sell exclusively to a restricted mailing list. "Russian River Pinots are deeply textured wines with dark fruits," he says, adding that "we make really ripe wines but we try not to get too ripe." There is also, of course, a good amount of Chardonnay produced in Russian River.

The terrain in Russian River Valley varies from flat expanses near the river to gently rolling hills. Soils vary, alluvial in the flood plain immediately around the river, sandstone, granite, or sandy loam elsewhere. There is more homogeneity to the west of Sebastopol, where soils are based on the so-called Goldridge loam. Just to the south of the Russian River Valley is the Petaluma gap, where a break in the mountains allows cool air to sweep from the Pacific across to San Francisco Bay, providing lots of fog and an important cooling influence.

Penetration by coastal fog is the important climatic influence; indeed, there have been attempts to redefine the boundaries of the AVA to confine it to the area covered by the fogs. Resulting from proximity to the ocean,

The Middle Reach of Russian River running along Westside Road is a flat flood plain. Russian River is behind the trees.

the western side of the AVA is cooler than the eastern. Overall the coolest part of the valley is the sub-AVA of Green Valley at the southern end. Today there are more than 15,000 acres of vineyards in Russian River Valley, with Chardonnay as the lead variety, followed by Pinot Noir; together they are close to three quarters of all plantings. It is fair to say these are not delicate wines; the style fairly bursts with fruit.

If I were compelled to use just a single word to describe the Pinot Noir of Russian River, it would be "sumptuous." The fruits are almost always forward, the impression on the palate is rich, tannins are rarely obvious. But vineyard differences come through the rich style. Russian River may have as many individual vineyard designations for its Pinot Noirs as anywhere on the West Coast. The highly varied soil types make any general grouping rather difficult. Together with variations in exposure to fog and general aspect of the land, not to mention clones and the age of the vines, the individual site acquires increased importance.

If you ask winegrowers to disentangle which of these influences are the more important, they shrug and say, "all of the above." But although they are certainly sensitive to variations in the quality and style of wines that come from different vineyard sources, you rarely hear anyone try to relate that quality or style to the specifics of the soil type as they might in Burgundy. You get the impression that climate is at least a more identifiable factor. Indeed, the most important single factor may be the hours of fog, which determine the daily growing temperature.

Several top vineyards lie to the west of Russian River in the area known to locals as "True Sonoma Coast," to distinguish it from the broad AVA. A

Heavy rains in 2017 flooded many vineyards along Russian River.

new AVA, Fort Ross-Seaview, has been created in this area, and identifies what is the coolest climate in the North Coast. There are only a few wineries in the area, but several producers in the better known valleys of Sonoma or in Napa own vineyards or purchase grapes to make Sonoma Coast cuvées of Pinot Noir or Chardonnay. Generally these are the most restrained of their cuvées. This is regarded as the coming area for Burgundian varieties.

Chardonnay in Napa and Sonoma

The Judgment of Paris tasting made it seem that either Cabernet Sauvignon or Chardonnay might become the major grape of Napa, and for a while Napa was equally well known for both. But Cabernet achieved greater success (and perhaps more to the point, greater prices), to the point at which it can be a financial sacrifice to plant anything other than Cabernet in Napa. More recently, many producers have come around to the view that Napa is really too warm for Chardonnay. "It's too warm for white varieties north of Oak Knoll," is a common view. There's agreement that the best Chardonnays come from Coombsville (south of Napa), Carneros (linking Napa and Sonoma), and Sonoma.

Chardonnay is Sonoma's most important grape variety, and is grown in all the sub AVAs. Like Pinot Noir, Russian River is the best known area. One of the best areas in Russian River for Chardonnay is Chalk Hill, which has a 12-24 inch layer of white volcanic ash. This is very depleted of nutrients and has similar drainage properties to chalk. "For the most part in Chalk Hill you see a more traditional style because the soils and temperatures are suitable for it. In Sonoma Coast you see a more modern style, fresher, crisper, brighter, with less oak. This is partly due to the soils, but more to the climate, especially the wind that funnels through the Petaluma Gap, which makes it several degrees cooler on average than Chalk Hill," explains winemaker Justin Seidenfeld at Rodney Strong.

The style of Chardonnay from Napa or Sonoma used to be very rich: full bodied and buttery, often with lots of vanillin, usually showing a strong oak influence. There are still Chardonnays in what might be called the traditional style, but there is an increasing move to a more restrained style, driven more by citrus than by stone fruits, with less new oak influence, and with malolactic fermentation fully or partially blocked to maintain fresh acidity. I would not go quite so far as to call them mineral, but the top wines in this style are moving in that direction.

Several top vineyards lie to the west of Russian River in the area known to locals as "True Sonoma Coast," to distinguish it from the broad AVA. A new AVA, Fort Ross-Seaview, has been created in this area, and identifies what is the coolest climate in the North Coast, but has not really come into general use: you are more likely to see just Sonoma Coast on the label.

There are only a few wineries in the area, but a producer's physical location is not necessarily a guide to the source of Chardonnay, as many producers in Napa or elsewhere in Sonoma own vineyards or purchase grapes to make Sonoma Coast cuvées of Chardonnay (or Pinot Noir). This is regarded as the coming area for Burgundian varieties.

Generally these are the most restrained of their cuvées, with an evidently leaner style than from other areas. The telltale that the wines come from the New World is usually higher alcohol than European wines along with a greater viscosity on the palate.

Cabernet Sauvignon in Sonoma

My recollection of the first Cabernet Sauvignons I tasted from Sonoma in the seventies is that they were distinctly leaner than Napa, not so surprising given Sonoma's slightly cooler climate. (Those wines would have come from valley floor sites that today would probably not be regarded as optimal for Cabernet.) That leaner quality does not seem to be true today; certainly as judged by alcohol levels, the Cabernets of Sonoma are right up there with Napa. "Sonoma even to a greater degree than Napa has more vagaries in climate and terroir. It probably was true that Sonoma Cabernet was leaner than Napa in the seventies but not so much now. There is more knowledge now about where to plant Cabernet, we know it needs to be in the warmer sites on hillsides, it used to be on the valley floor," says winemaker Richard Arrowood, who was there right at the beginning, producing Cabernet Sauvignon first at Chateau St. Jean later at Arrowood, and now at his latest venture, Amapola Creek. Part of the reason the difference has apparently lessened may be the increased concentration on growing Cab-

The Monte Rosso vineyard occupies a peak at 1,200 ft in the Mayacamas Mountains with direct exposure to San Pablo Bay, fifteen miles away. Courtesy Louis Martini.

ernet in mountain vineyards, which may be more similar between Sonoma and Napa than are the valley floors.

Perhaps because of that initial leanness, there seems to have been more concern to soften the Cabernet with other varieties in Sonoma. "Green bean character in Cabernet Sauvignon was typical in the 1990s. Then Parker came along and it became unacceptable," says Rob Davis, who has been making wine at Jordan Vineyards since the seventies.

"The wines made in the seventies were fairly extracted; there wasn't this 'I want to take it home and drink it tonight'—you really had to lay them down. We thought that blending would make a softer wine," says Margo Van Staaveren, who has been at Chateau St. Jean throughout. This was the impetus for Chateau St. Jean's introduction of Cinq Cepages in 1990, a wine made from all five classic Bordeaux varieties. "The idea was to have approachability, accessibility, and ageability; they weren't accessible wines we made in the seventies," she recollects. "I have Napa envy, they get the lush rich textures that are not so easy to come by in Sonoma," she adds.

Opinions have oscillated on blends versus varietals. "The early vineyard designates were all 100% Cabernet Sauvignon. There weren't a lot of the other varieties—when there was a blend the cheapest variety was the Cabernet Sauvignon!—you couldn't find the other varieties," Richard Arrowood recollects about the early days at Chateau St. Jean. Things went in the other direction at Arrowood, where Richard made the wines through the nineties. The two top wines were the monovarietal Cabernet Sauvignon from the Monte Rosso vineyard and the Réserve Spéciale, a blend from several vineyards.

The rusty red appearance of the iron-rich soils lives up to Monte Rosso's name.

Probably the most famous vineyard in Sonoma, the Monte Rosso ranch has 250 acres of vines spread across the peak of the mountain with views across to San Pablo Bay. As the name suggests, it has rocky, red volcanic soils; most of the topsoils are 18-24 inches deep, based on pure rock. Exposure to the bay ensures cool breezes all day and keeps up the acidity in the berries.

The vineyard was originally planted by Emanuel Goldstein in the early 1880s with a wide mix of varieties. It was wiped out by phylloxera and replanted in 1890, when Zinfandel became a significant part of the plantings. Some of these old vines still remain as blocks of Zinfandel or field blends with Alicante and Beaunoir.

When Louis Martini took over the vineyard in 1938, they concentrated on Zinfandel and Cabernet Sauvignon. (In the interim, they called the wine Monte Rosso Chianti.) Among the plantings from 1938, the surviving Cabernet Sauvignon vines are probably the oldest Cabernet in the USA. Now owned by Gallo, grapes are sold to several producers, but a common thread in the wines is a sense of fine structure supporting elegant fruits.

Old Vines Zinfandel

Brought from Italy in the nineteenth century, Zinfandel is one of the longest established grapes in California. At 10% of the total crush, it's behind only Chardonnay and Cabernet Sauvignon. But it's a very mixed bag.

A major proportion goes into White Zinfandel, basically a light, sweet, rosé. This originated by an accident at Sutter Home in the 1970s, when Bob Trinchero was making a dry white Zinfandel, but fermentation stuck,

Zinfandel bunches ripen unevenly. Courtesy Lodi winegrowers.

Zinfandel vines in Sonoma's Monte Rosso vineyard are more than one hundred years old.

so the wine was bottled slightly sweet. It was such a success that by 1987 it was the best selling premium wine in the United States.

Zinfandel made as a conventional dry red wine accounts for a minority of production. The peculiarity of Zinfandel is that bunches always ripen unevenly, in fact so unevenly that a single bunch may contain grapes of widely varying sizes in states varying from green to desiccated. The ripest grapes accumulate a lot of sugar, so alcohol is always high, and the greenest grapes contribute acidity.

A typical dry Zinfandel is likely to have alcohol around 16%, with intense aromatics, an impression of sweetness coming from the high alcohol and aromatics, and a hint of piquancy. I suppose this might be regarded as its typicity, but personally I find it so overwhelming that it's hard to see much difference in different wines.

The exception comes from old Zinfandel, often in fact very old, meaning vines of more than a century in age. Plots of very gnarled head-pruned old vines can be seen all over California: these are very often old Zinfandel. In fact, given the way vineyards were planted a century ago, they are rarely exclusively Zinfandel, but more often a field blend in which Zinfandel predominates, but which also includes Carignan, Alicante Bouschet, and other varieties common to the period.

These can make some remarkable wines. In fact, I am inclined to the view that Zinfandel makes interesting wine *only* when the vines approach a hundred years of age (a characteristic it shares with Carignan in the South of France). The naturally low yield of the old vines is needed to get flavor variety.

A few producers specialize in cuvées of old vines Zinfandel, but I suspect that the differences between the cuvées, interesting though they are, owe less to terroir and more to the age of the vines and to variations in the field blend. At this level, the sweet high-toned aromatics of Zinfandel recede into the background as a counterpoise to the black fruit flavors on the palate.

Santa Cruz Mountains

The doyen of Cabernet Sauvignon in California in the modern era might not be in Napa or Sonoma at all, but in the Santa Cruz Mountains just south of San Francisco, where microclimates vary to the point at which on successive ridges (within five miles as the crow flies), you can find the famous Ridge Montebello vineyard where Cabernet Sauvignon triumphs, and Fogarty's vineyards of Pinot Noir.

Wine production started at Ridge in the nineteenth century, although it lacks the continuous history of Beaulieu or Inglenook, having closed during Prohibition; it was revived in the 1960s. Another couple of peaks along the mountain range, Martin Ray established his winery in the 1940s. After he left in 1970, it became the Mount Eden vineyard. Both Ridge and Mount Eden have a long history with Cabernet Sauvignon. The vines for both properties originated with a selection brought from Margaux in the nineteenth century by Emmet Rixford (no one is sure whether the wines actually came from Château Margaux or merely from the Margaux appellation). The original plantings are still propagated by selection massale at both wineries.

A cool climate for Cabernet Sauvignon, the Santa Cruz mountain appellation has roughly equal amounts of Pinot Noir, Chardonnay, and Cabernet Sauvignon (and then a mix of other varieties). With vineyards at altitudes from 1,300 to 2,600 ft, exposed to cooling influences from the Pacific only a few miles away, the style is more moderate than Napa or Sonoma. "Santa Cruz is more soil-driven than fruit-driven and appeals to a more Eurocentric style. Alcohol levels here are usually lower," says winemaker Jeffrey Patterson at Mount Eden.

The topsoils in the mountains are thin, based on shale. At Ridge, the unusual terroir has a fractured layer of limestone overlaid with green stone (a highly friable sedimentary rock). The vine roots penetrate easily through the green stone and can go into the limestone. Is it the terroir that's responsible for the minerality in the wines or just better retention of acidity due to

From the steep, elevated vineyards in Santa Cruz, there are views over San Francisco Bay fifty miles to the north and west.

the cooler climate? The wines are long lived. "The natural instinct of the vineyards here is to make a 25 year wine," says Jeffrey Patterson. And that is certainly true of Ridge, where the Cabernets begin to develop well after a decade and may last for three or more decades. Ridge's Montebello vineyard is one of the most famous in California, and produces one of the longest-lived wines.

The modern history of Ridge began when a group of engineers from Stanford University bought the property on the Santa Cruz Mountains south of San Francisco in 1959 and started producing Cabernet Sauvignon from vines that had been planted in the 1940s. Over the next few years they expanded the vineyard area from 15 to 45 acres (introducing Zinfandel from 1964), and production grew to about 3,000 cases. Paul Draper, a Stanford philosophy graduate who had been making wine in Chile, joined in 1969 because he was so impressed with the 1962 and 1964 Cabernets (both monovarietal). "It was the first time I tasted California wine, outside of the old Inglenook and Beaulieu wines, with the complexity of Bordeaux. Those two wines were the reason why I joined Ridge. The wines were completely natural," he says.

Ridge has several different vineyards all planted along the Monte Bello Ridge, which runs roughly northwest to south-east. Both terroir and climate are different from Napa and Sonoma on the North Coast. This explains the moderate character of the wines. "We are too cool here to do what Napa is doing and anyway I don't like the style. My reference point was Château Latour, until Bordeaux began to change. We stayed with the style of moderate alcohol. For the first forty years it was 12.9%, now it is around 13.1%," Paul says.

Because the vineyards are located literally on a ridge, every parcel has a slightly different exposure and has been planted accordingly with the intention of achieving even ripening. "When I say fully ripe I get into a

Vineyards on Santa Cruz mountains look out over Silicon Valley to the east. Courtesy Ridge Vineyards.

definition that has become—I shouldn't say controversial—but California has a totally different interpretation of what ripeness is. In the Santa Cruz mountains the average temperature is the same as Bordeaux but the nights are cooler and for that reason we retain acidity much better than elsewhere in California, such as Napa. We have never added acidity but sometimes we have had to precipitate it out."

Monte Bello is a blend, and perhaps not surprisingly considering Paul's traditional imperatives, closer to Bordeaux in its varietal composition than to a Napa Cabernet. The transition took a while, from the monovarietal of the early sixties, to a wine with over 90% Cabernet Sauvignon in the eighties, and then to a range over the past two decades from a minimum of 56% to a maximum of 85%. Merlot is always the second most important variety, with smaller amounts of Petit Verdot and Cabernet Franc. Monte Bello is a long-lived wine; Paul thinks it begin to show its characteristics around 9-12 years of age, and develops until it is 20 or 30 years old. As for really old vintages, the 1974 was only just past its peak at 35 years of age, and the 1964 was rather tertiary but still enjoyable at 45 years. I can't help but wonder how much the moderate style of the wines is a key factor in ensuring such longevity.

Soils in Santa Cruz Mountains are shale or sandstone, generally without much clay. Perhaps because the area is circumscribed, Santa Cruz is one of the few AVAs to be relatively unaffected by politics. Vineyards have to be above the fog line. Here the pattern is the reverse of elsewhere with morning sun and afternoon fog. Thomas Fogarty was the pioneer for Pinot Noir, but now has been followed by several others. The wines tend to

An old lime kiln gave the clue that this was the terroir for Pinot Noir where Calera was established. Courtesy Calera.

spicy black fruits with good tannic support, and age well for up to two decades.

Limestone in Mount Harlan

An hour or so farther south on Mount Harlan are the vineyards where Josh Jensen founded Calera Wines in 1972 when he found limestone. "Trespassers will be transmogrificated," says the sign at the entrance to Calera, an indication that Josh Jensen has lost none of his feisty character with age. As an avowed Burgundian, Josh believes that nothing but limestone terroir can make great Pinot Noir. "For me the definition of great wine is that it's extremely complex. The classic great Pinot Noirs are grown on limestone soils—I took as my theoretical start on Pinot Noir that they were great because they were grown on limestone. All of the vineyards here are on limestone," he told me. That simple statement belies a long and dedicated search for limestone terroir in California.

After spending 1969 and 1970 working in Burgundy, including a spell at Romanée Conti, Josh Jensen returned to the United States with the ambition of growing great Pinot Noir. He looked for limestone terroir all over California, and finally found a marker in the form of an old lime kiln (used to produce lime at a quarry) on Mount Harlan. The name of his company reflects these origins; Calera is the Spanish for lime kiln. At almost 2,200 ft elevation, the vineyards are among the highest (and coolest) in the United States. The cool climate comes not only from the elevation but also from cold breezes and fog direct from the Pacific, only a few miles away. The vineyards are well isolated from all other vineyards, the nearest being the Santa Cruz Mountain AVA fifty miles to the north. Calera's unique quality is recognized in the existence of the Mount Harlan AVA in which it is the only winery.

Spread over more than 600 acres on the mountain, there are now six separate Pinot Noir vineyards. Most of the plantings are the Calera selection, which came from 18 original vines at Chalone. (No one will comment any more on the old story that the original source of these vines was cuttings liberated from Romanée Conti.) In spite of the cool climate and the limestone soils, usually it's necessary to acidify. Jensen's winemaking may be more Burgundian than the Burgundians: there's no protracted cold soak, most grapes go into the vat as uncrushed whole clusters, fermentation occurs naturally by indigenous yeasts, and continues until the cap falls.

Overall it's just a fraction warmer here than in Burgundy, but the key to character and ageability, Josh says, is the soil. Tasting a horizontal of Calera's single vineyard wines is an exercise comparable to traveling from the Côte de Beaune to the Côte de Nuits; there is no mistaking the differences between vineyards. The wines have savory and even herbaceous elements in the Old World style, but the forwardness of the sweet ripe fruits and the high alcohol is New World.

Vintages

Vintages have been more erratic since 2000, perhaps a consequence of global warming, but after some real ups and downs ending in the difficult 2011 vintage, there has been a stream of good vintages. "Critics find 2012 to be better than 2014 but I think that's because 2012 followed the miserable 2011 vintage, and 2014 followed the 2013, which is the greatest vintage we've had in fifty years. 2007 and 2010 would be next (after 2013), and then 2014," says winemaker Peter Heitz at Turnbull.

2017	Odd season with alternating temperatures, but good end to season suggests high quality although low yields. Wildfires at end of season were a problem for grapes that had not been harvested.
2016	Regarded as a perfect growing season and very promising.
2015	Signs are promising. Very small vintage but rich: flavor is at the forefront here, whereas tannins were at the forefront in 2013. Barrel samples show lovely aromatics.

2014	92	Precocious Spring, dry summer, and early harvest gave strong Cabernets, but not as tannic as 2013. Often the most aromatic character of 2012-2014.	14.9%
2013	94	Touted as a great vintage for Cabernet from an ideal season with dry, sunny conditions; the downside is high alcohol. Wines are intense, rich, and muscular: many will require some years to come around. The strong tannins of the vintage in Napa Valley are especially evident in Oakville. For Pinot Noir in Sonoma, not as good as 2012 or 2014, which are the best years for a very long time.	15.2%
2012	93	Return to classic conditions with well-structured Cabernets. Very well received with relief after several difficult vintages. Wines can be elegant, without the raw power of 2013.	14.5%
2011	86	A problem vintage because of cool weather and rain, giving lower alcohol levels and lighter wines; difficult to get the right balance with ripeness. Regarded in the region as a very poor for reds.	13.7%
2010	88	Reduced in size by problems in Spring, with cool conditions followed by heat in late summer. Said to be elegant, but sometimes a bit lacking in character.	14.1%
2009	89	Mild summer, even conditions, wines a bit on lighter side tending to softness for early drinking.	14.5%
2008	90	Reduced in size by Spring frosts, giving concentrated wines that may take time to come around.	14.8%
2007	94	Lush, opulent wines in Napa's modern style, well received and universally praised.	14.7%
2006	90	Slightly lighter vintage that did not attract much attention.	14.8%
2005	92	Cooler, longer growing season gave structured wines. Questions is whether fruits will outlive tannins in the long run.	14.5%
2004	91	Early harvest resulted from heat in August. Big, rich wines, maturing relatively early.	14.9%
2003	88	Irregular conditions with cool growing season followed by hot September, generally for drinking early.	14.4%
2002	92	Classic in the new Napa style tending to richness and opulence.	14.6%
2001	93	Even, long growing season gave well-structured wines	14.3%

		thought to be long-lived, but I find them a bit lacking in generosity.	
2000	86	Summer heat waves followed by October rains gave tight acidic wines that were not very well received.	13.8%

Vintages are rated on 100 point scale. Fourth column shows average alcohol in Napa Cabernets.

Visiting the Region

Napa Valley has changed enormously since the start, when there were sporadic wineries up and down route 29, and a few on the Silverado Trail, and you could stop in almost anywhere for a tasting. Today the wineries are choc a bloc, and on a long weekend or during peak summer, the road can be jammed by limos out from San Francisco for the day.

Virtually all wineries sell wine at the cellar door; indeed, for smaller, high-end producers, this represents the majority of sales. Most wineries have tasting rooms, and most now make a charge for tasting. This varies from a nominal cost ($10-20) to cover the wine being poured to something more significant, especially for special bottlings. The profiles show the *minimum* charge for a tasting. Many wineries offer a variety of tastings at increasing price levels depending on the number and age of wines being poured. Sometimes any charge is credited back if you buy wines.

Many wineries require an appointment: this usually results in a more extended visit, typically from 60 to 90 minutes, starting with a tour of the vineyards and winery, concluding with a tasting. Typically the charges here are higher, and the visit is regarded as a profit center for the winery. It's usually adequate to make appointments a week or so ahead, but a month or so in advance is a good idea for busy periods. (The cellarpass online system is used to make reservations for more than 200 of the wineries: see www.cellarpass.com.) Pressure for appointments is created by restrictions limiting how many visitors a winery is allowed to receive each day. It is fair to say that the atmosphere has become much more commercial in Napa Valley in recent years. It's still possible to drive up the valley and stop to taste without an appointment, but it is fair to say that this excludes many of the more interesting producers.

Downtown Napa is a bit south of most wineries, although it takes only about 30 minutes to drive up to Calistoga at the northern end of the valley (somewhat longer on busy weekends or during rush hour). Yountville is a central base for visiting wineries all along the valley, and has several hotels and restaurants, as does St. Helena, towards the northern end. Between Yountville and St. Helena, the Oakville Grocery on route 29 is a good spot to grab lunch. It's generally less crowded driving along the Silverado Trail than along route 29. Allow much more time for visiting wineries either to the west or to the east of the valley proper, as roads are narrow, steep, and winding.

Sonoma is more relaxed, if only because most of the wineries are off the beaten track, on roads running well off the thoroughfare of route 101. Appointments may be necessary, especially at smaller wineries, but charges are likely to be more modest. Given the greater dispersion of the wineries, the towns of Healdsburg, Santa Rosa, and Sonoma have clusters of tasting rooms, sometimes dedicated to individual wineries, sometimes representing groups of wineries, but it's fair to say that for most of the more interesting producers it is better to go to the winery.

It takes only about an hour to drive over the Mayacamas mountains between Napa and Sonoma, but it is certainly easier to visit producers in the valley where you are staying. Healdsburg is a central location for Sonoma as it provides an entrance to several subvalleys, especially Russian River. Santa Rosa is also fairly central; Sonoma is a little to the south of most wineries.

Many of the wineries in Napa and Sonoma have wine clubs, and may give preference to members for visits, as well as making certain wines available only to them by mail order. It is now also common for wines that are made only in small amounts to be available only at the winery. A typical pattern would be for an AVA wine to be in general distribution, but for single vineyard wines to be available only at the winery or through the wine club.

Profiles of Leading Estates

Napa	*49*
Sonoma	*112*
Carneros	*146*
Santa Cruz	*150*
Mount Harlan	*155*

Ratings	
***	Excellent producers defining the very best of the appellation
**	Top producers whose wines typify the appellation
*	Very good producers making wines of character that rarely disappoint

Symbols	
Address	Tasting room with especially warm welcome
Phone	Tastings/visits possible
Owner/winemaker/contact	By appointment only
Email	Minimum charge for tasting
Website	No visits
AVA	Sales directly at producer
Red White Reference wines	No direct sales
Second wine	Mailing list only
Grower-producer	
Negociant (or purchases grapes)	
Conventional viticulture	
Sustainable viticulture	
Organic	
Biodynamic	
ha=estate vineyards	
bottles=annual production	

Napa

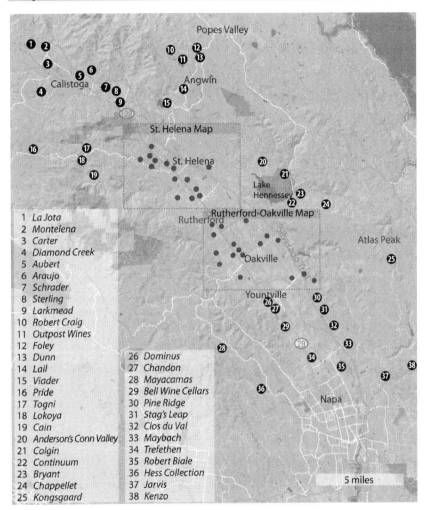

1 La Jota
2 Montelena
3 Carter
4 Diamond Creek
5 Aubert
6 Araujo
7 Schrader
8 Sterling
9 Larkmead
10 Robert Craig
11 Outpost Wines
12 Foley
13 Dunn
14 Lail
15 Viader
16 Pride
17 Togni
18 Lokoya
19 Cain
20 Anderson's Conn Valley
21 Colgin
22 Continuum
23 Bryant
24 Chappellet
25 Kongsgaard
26 Dominus
27 Chandon
28 Mayacamas
29 Bell Wine Cellars
30 Pine Ridge
31 Stag's Leap
32 Clos du Val
33 Maybach
34 Trefethen
35 Robert Biale
36 Hess Collection
37 Jarvis
38 Kenzo

St. Helena

1 Turley
2 Gallica
3 Freemark Abbey
4 Vineyard 29
5 Morlet
6 Beringer
7 Tor Kenward
8 Hourglass
9 Newton
10 Abreu
11 Spottswoode
12 Chase Cellars
13 HALL
14 Louis Martini
15 Heitz
16 Pahlmeyer
17 Corison
18 Flora Springs
19 Whitehall
20 Joseph Phelps

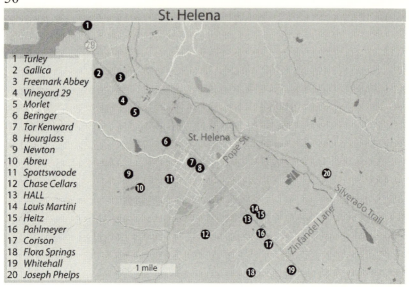

Rutherford-Oakville

1 ZD
2 Caymus
3 Alpha Omega
4 Grgich
5 Beaulieu
6 Inglenook
7 Staglin
8 Harlan
9 Peju Provence
10 St. Supery
11 Cakebread
12 Turnbull
13 Nickel & Nickel
14 Mondavi
15 Opus One
16 Silver Oak
17 Groth
18 B cellars
19 Plumpjack
20 Screaming Eagle
21 Dalla Valle
22 Far Niente
23 Kapcsandy
24 Sinskey
25 Shafer

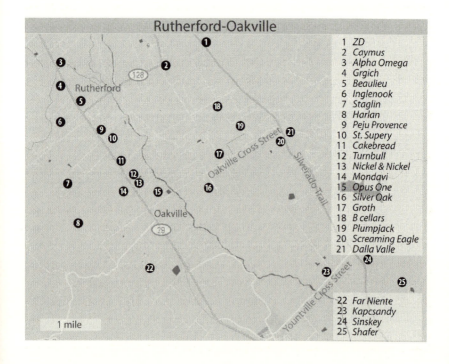

Abreu Vineyards ★★

📍 2366 Madrona Ave, St. Helena, CA 94574
📞 (1) 707 963 3465
👤 Brad Grimes or Nicole Burns
@ info@abreuvineyard.com
🌐 www.abreuvineyards.com
⬛ St. Helena
🍾 Madrona Ranch, Cabernet Sauvignon
🚫 ⓦ
🍇 81 acres; 12,000 bottles
[map p. 50]

David Abreu has long been famous as a grape grower. Many producers will tell you proudly that a cuvée comes from one of the Abreu vineyards, and Abreu grapes are behind a fair number of Napa's cult wines. Abreu has four properties, and he now keeps grapes from 20-25 acres for making his own wine.

It's hard to describe the mode of viticulture. "I don't keep up on all of the nomenclature around the different farming styles," says Brad Grimes. "We are not certified in any style of farming nor would we ever choose to define ourselves by one or all of those names. I can definitely say that we are unlike any other farming company...We farm all of our vineyards using organic materials, and, at Madrona Ranch, use a circular system of farming that incorporates animals that is more along the lines of biodynamic, although we are not following a manual. So, all of the [categories], with the exception of conventional. That is one thing we are not..."

The facility is a long branching tunnel into the hill, dug in 1979, extended in 1982, then finished in 2006. All the wine is made here in a long row of 2 ton fermenters. There's 100% new oak, 2-3 rackings, no fining: "no reason to fine at all," says winemaker Brad Grimes. Lots are picked when ready and then cofermented irrespective of variety. "One of the advantages of cofermentation is that you can usually balance out acid and alcohol. People tend to think that separating into lots and fermenting as such is more precise, instead of taking fruits that are ready together."

Each of the vineyards—Madrona (23 acres), Capella (6 acres), Thorevilos (20 acres), and Las Posadas (35 acres) on Howell Mountain—has all the Bordeaux varieties. Madrona Ranch in St. Helena is the most famous of the holdings, unusual for its red strip of ferrous soil. There's 65-70% Cabernet Sauvignon at Capella, 45-60% at the others, and some Malbec at Howell Mountain. There's extensive picking—6 passes through Madrona and 3-4 through the other vineyards—and lots that don't make it into the vineyard wines go into a general blend; below that it's sold off in bulk. "I don't get inspiration from Napa, I get it from Bordeaux," says Brad.

There are four single vineyard wines, and also one wine, Rothwell Hyde, that is blended from all the vineyards. Thorevilos is the most approachable, Capella is the most refined, Las Posadas (Howell Mountain) surprisingly soft at first ("Howell Mountain doesn't have to be hard") until the structure kicks in, and Madrona is the most profound and complete ("What you see about Madrona is the beautiful lively backbone.") For me it has the freshness of Cabernet Franc and the backbone of Cabernet Sauvignon. "California in a Bordeaux style," was the comment of a Bordeaux winemaker at a tasting.

Alpha Omega Winery

1155 Mee Ln, Rutherford, CA 94574

(1) 707 963 9999

info@aowinery.com

www.aowinery.com

Rutherford

Napa Cabernet Sauvignon

$25

0 acres; 144,000 bottles

[map p. 50]

A relatively new enterprise, established in 2006, by Robin and Michelle Baggett who had been grape growers at the Tolouse winery in San Luis Obispo, Alpha Omega operates on an unusual basis: its wines do not go into general distribution but are sold almost entirely at the winery or through the wine club or directly to restaurants. Right on route 29, the premises are designed with entertainment in mind, with a large well staffed tasting room and an outside terrace overlooking the vineyards for sitting and tasting.

Aside from the immediately surrounding vineyard of Sauvignon Blanc, all grapes are sourced from growers. With a Swiss winemaker who comes from Bordeaux, and Michel Rolland as consultant, the objective is to produce wines reflecting both European and Californian influences. The focus is on reds, with 18 different cuvées, including eight single vineyard Cabernets (including many from the most famous vineyards of Napa).

I would describe the house style as very rich, full-force Napa, from the Napa Chardonnay, which is full, fat, buttery, and nutty, to the Proprietary Red (a Bordeaux blend, with varieties that change each year but with Cabernet Sauvignon as the major variety), which is smooth and unctuous. The overt juiciness of style for the varietal Cabernets is more reserved because of structure in the background. There's a steady increase in fruit intensity matched by a greater sense of texture from the relatively straightforward Proprietary Red through the more structured Napa Cabernet (which contains some Petit Verdot and Cabernet Franc but no Merlot) to the deeper single vineyard Cabernets (which are monovarietals). The sheer richness of the fruits makes all of the cuvées more or less immediately approachable.

Diageo

Beaulieu Vineyards *

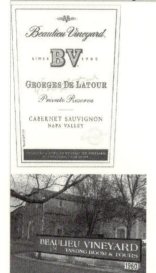

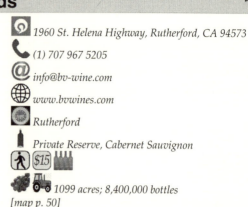

1960 St. Helena Highway, Rutherford, CA 94573
(1) 707 967 5205
info@bv-wine.com
www.bvwines.com
Rutherford
Private Reserve, Cabernet Sauvignon
$15
1099 acres; 8,400,000 bottles
[map p. 50]

Perhaps it's no more than sentimental to include Beaulieu in a list of top Cabernet producers, but it has played such a significant role in the history of Cabernet Sauvignon in Napa Valley. After George de Latour established Beaulieu in the historic heart of Rutherford, the Private Reserve was one of a mere handful of top quality wines made in Napa Valley. André Tchelistcheff, who made the wine from 1938 until his retirement in 1973, became a legend. Although erratic because there were two bottlings, one brilliant and one not so good, the 1974 was one of the top wines of that legendary vintage.

Beaulieu turned away from quality under the ownership of Heublein, beginning its expansion into the broader market; sold on in 1987, became just one of Diageo's labels. Then in 2015 it was sold to Treasury along with most of Diageo's wineries. The tasting room is in a historic building, but the modern winery behind more resembles an oil refinery. However, there are now plans to move production of all but the very top-end wines to Treasury's main winery at Beringer just north of Napa. Perhaps it's an indication of where the focus now lies that in 2017 Beaulieu announced an important initiative: to introduce new labels emphasizing its position as a Napa "Grand Cru" producer!

The Private Reserve today is a workmanlike Cabernet, but does not have that special refinement of the historic classic vintages. This is not surprising considering that the plots in the To Kalon vineyard that had been part of the great Private Reserves were sold to Andy Beckstoffer (from whom several producers now purchase grapes for bottlings of cult Cabernets). There are several ranges of wines at quality levels extending to the entry-level BV Coastal Estates (named for their origin in the Central Coast). The wines are well made and serviceable.

Bronco Wine Cellars

Bell Wine Cellars *

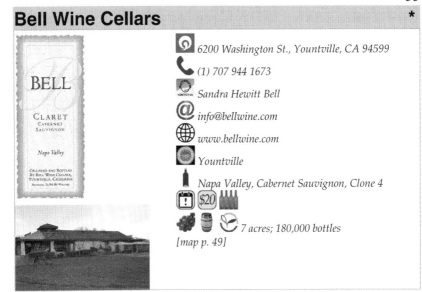

6200 Washington St., Yountville, CA 94599

(1) 707 944 1673

Sandra Hewitt Bell

info@bellwine.com

www.bellwine.com

Yountville

Napa Valley, Cabernet Sauvignon, Clone 4

$20

7 acres; 180,000 bottles

[map p. 49]

After spending the 1980s at Beaulieu Vineyards, Anthony Bell started his own winery in 1991 by producing Cabernet Sauvignon from clone 6 in borrowed facilities, moving into his own winery in Yountville in 1998. His style is to make wines with a European sensibility. He was involved in Beaulieu's project for characterizing different clones of Cabernet Sauvignon, and today he produces monovarietal Cabernet Sauvignons from several different clones, as well as a blend with the classic Bordeaux varieties, and a "claret" that also includes some Syrah and Petite Syrah.

Three barrels for each individual clone give around 900 bottles for each of clones 7, 4, 6, and 337. The wines from clone 7 and clone 4 have similar profiles, but on clone 7 you see the fruits first, and this reverses on clone 4 where you see the herbal influence first. All the wines show an impressive sense of the tradition of Cabernet Sauvignon, but the most striking difference is between clone 337, which shows the most lush character—the Dijon clone of Cabernet Sauvignon, you might say—and clone 6, which has the most traditional austerity. The main focus here is on the 6 cuvées of pure varietal Cabernet Sauvignons, but there are also Merlot, Syrah, Chardonnay, and Sauvignon Blanc.

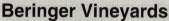
Treasury Wine Estates

Beringer Vineyards   **

2000 Main Street, St. Helena, CA 94574

(1) 707 963 7115

cs_beringer@beringer.com

www.beringer.com

St. Helena

Napa Cabernet Sauvignon

Napa, Luminus Chardonnay

 $25

9400 acres; 144,000,000 bottles
[map p. 50]

Beringer is the longest continuously operating winery in Napa, founded in 1885 by two brothers from Mainz in Germany (which explains the style of their Victorian mansion, the Rhine house). The original purchase was 175 acres. Beringer accumulated 1,600 acres by 1971, when the family sold the company, which moved through various owners to become part of Treasury wine estates. The wines are made at a industrial-looking winery across the street from the historic house, which is now the tasting room. The winery is now the center for Treasury's high-end production, and makes some of the wines under the Beaulieu and Sterling labels, as well as Chateau St. Jean in Sonoma. (Bulk wines are produced at an even larger winery in Paso Robles.)

Although Beringer now produces around 12 million cases in total, the luxury division accounts for about 300,000 cases. "The 300,000 probably take more effort to produce than the 12 million," Mark Beringer says dryly. He is Jacob Beringer's great great grandson; having previously worked elsewhere, he became winemaker here in 2015. "Coming in here there was an established style that needed to be maintained. We were pioneers in the style of Napa and would not want to tinker with something that is successful, so the way we innovate is to try new styles," he says.

Beringer divides its wines into several series: the top-level series are the Private Reserve (Cabernet Sauvignon and Chardonnay), Single Vineyards (seven Cabernets from sites all over Napa, available only at the winery), and most recently the Distinction Series. The difference between the Private Reserve and the Distinction Series reflects changes at Beringer and in the region generally. "Private Reserve Chardonnay is a big buttery wine with large amounts of oak, from a warm region (Oakville), and goes through full MLF. Luminus (in the Distinction series) was designed to be a counterpart: leaner with much less MLF, emphasizing citrus and floral, more food friendly. This has been a trend for probably ten years. Distinction Cabernet Sauvignon had the first vintage in 2014 and the key to this wine is that we tried to create a Cabernet that is a bit more polished and modern, with bright fruits and high toned characteristics from the oak. Quantum (a Bordeaux blend) is sourced from a lot of the same estates as the Private Reserve Cabernet, but we select the lots that have a broader tannin profile and will be more approachable. We want Distinction to be definitely its own style," Mark explains.

Beringer is big on Knights Valley, and two of its wines from there reflect its stylistic range: the Cabernet Sauvignon is a blend, with broad flavors, but the Reserve represents a pure Cabernet, very fine and precise. Of course, the most famous wine is the Private Reserve Cabernet Sauvignon; "It comes primarily from mountain fruit, it is made to age, and will easily last 25 years," Mark says. It is indeed an enormously powerful wine: personally I would not even start a Private Reserve for ten years, and twenty might be better. The difficulty with Beringer is to decide which style suits you: the power of the Private Reserve, the modernity but more muted character of Distinction, or the precision of the single vineyard Cabernets.

Bryant Family Vineyard ★★★

1567 Sage Canyon Rd., St. Helena, CA 94574
(1) 314 231 8066
Brady Mitchell
info@bryantwines.com
www.bryantwines.com
St. Helena
Bryant, Cabernet Sauvignon
DB4

12 acres; 50,000 bottles
[map p. 49]

Don Bryant purchased the land for his vineyard in a striking spot on Pritchard Hill overlooking Lake Hennessey. "I bought the top of a mountain for a home site and decided it would be fun to start a vineyard. I looked for the best vineyard within 10-15 miles of the house. There was a vineyard close by, planted with Cabernet Sauvignon and Chardonnay, and run down. All the old winemakers said it was the best vineyard around. Grapes had previously been sold to Caymus and others. I made an unsolicited bid in 1986 for 12 acres, and closed the deal within 24 hours," he recalls.

The first vintage was in 1992, with Helen Turley as the winemaker. Early vintages were propelled into instant success. Since then, there have been several winemakers, with changes in style depending on using techniques ranging from barrel fermentation to greater maceration and extraction. "Helen's wines were very reflective of vintage, perfumed and delicate in 1996, massive in 1997," says a later winemaker, Helen Keplinger.

The vineyard is on west-facing volcanic soils, with a cooling influence from the lake just below. It is divided into 22 blocks spread out over 12 acres, and is planted exclusively with Cabernet Sauvignon (a mixture of Spottswoode clone and 337). The character of Bryant is maintained by declassifying lots into a second wine, called DB4. "Wines that are declassified to DB4 are less concentrated, and the tannins are less refined. DB4 is not necessarily shorter lived than Bryant," says Helen Keplinger. Both Bryant and DB4 are 100% Cabernet Sauvignon, and the latest development is an extension into a Bordeaux blend, called Bettina after Don's wife, coming from David Abreu's vineyards at Madrona Ranch, Thorevilos, and Lucia Howell Mountain; the inaugural vintage is 2009. Bettina is produced in roughly the same quantity as Bryant (around 1,500 cases).

Cakebread Cellars   *

8300 St. Helena Highway, Rutherford, CA 94573

(1) 800 588 0298

James Howard

cellars@cakebread.com

www.cakebread.com

Rutherford

Anderson Valley, Two Creeks Vineyard Pinot Noir

Napa Valley Cabernet Sauvignon

Carneros, Reserve Chardonnay

$25

1200 acres; 1,800,000 bottles

[map p. 50]

Cakebread cellars started more or less by accident when Jack and Dolores Cakebread bought a 22 acre ranch in Rutherford in 1972. The first wine was the 1973 Chardonnay, with only 157 cases produced, released in 1974. The first Cabernet was the 1974 vintage, released in 1976. The winery was built in 1974 and enlarged in 1977; it was replaced by a new building in 1980, and has been continuously expanded ever since. By 1979 the family became fully professionally involved when Bruce Cakebread joined with a degree in oenology from UC Davis. A continuing program of vineyard purchases expanded production into Carneros, Howell Mountain, and Anderson Valley. Estate vineyards provide about 60% of all grapes. There are about twenty wines in all, but the flagship remains the Napa Valley Chardonnay, which accounts for half of all production; with another 30% in the Napa Sauvignon Blanc, Cakebread is decidedly a white wine house, but in reds also produces several cuvées of Pinot Noir and Cabernet Sauvignon as well as some other varieties.

There are some distinct geographical differences in sources for different varieties. Aside from the general Napa Valley bottlings, Chardonnay comes from Carneros, Pinot Noir comes from Anderson Valley, and Cabernet Sauvignon comes from Howell Mountain. There used to be both Pinot Noir and Chardonnay from both Carneros and Anderson Valley, but "The Pinot Noir was exceptional from Anderson Valley and the Chardonnay was just good," says winemaker Julianne Laks, "so now we've focused on one place for each variety." The style for Chardonnay limits MLF, typically to less than a third, but compensates by barrel fermentation followed by battonage to increase texture; it becomes richer going from the Napa to the Carneros to the single vineyard Cuttings Wharf. New oak is under a third. "We've always done this with whites, I'm really pleased we stood our ground, people are coming back to our style," Julianne says. I would describe it as a halfway house between the full, rich style of the past, and the more angular style of some recent Napa Chardonnays. The Pinot Noirs show quite an earthy style for Carneros.

The Napa Cabernet has a refined texture, and the sense of precision increases in the Dancing Bear Ranch cuvée from Howell Mountain; the most powerful Cabernet is the Benchland Select, a barrel selection from two vineyards in Oakville and Rutherford. A sense of moderation typifies the house. There's an effort at Cakebread to keep alcohol down. "We've been very successful with whites by growing the grapes to get maturity at lower Brix. With red grapes it's more difficult. It's not fun having a wine with too much alcohol," Julianne says.

Caymus Vineyards ★

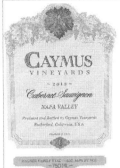

8700 Conn Creek Road, P.O. Box 268, Rutherford, CA 94573

(1) 707 967 3010

Lynda Sakai

info@caymus.com

www.wagnerfamilyofwine.com

Rutherford

Special Selection

$50

74 acres; 360,000 bottles

[map p. 50]

The Wagners have been involved in growing grapes in Napa for a long time. "Napa was a different place when we started in the 1880s, then we had phylloxera and Prohibition, and that put the family out of the business. They planted a litany of crops, the best was prunes, so I grew up around prunes and prune dehydration. In 1966 my father pulled up the prunes and planted grapes," recalls Chuck Wagner.

Caymus Vineyards started in 1972 with a release of 240 cases of Cabernet Sauvignon. Today Wagner has expanded into a group of family businesses, with wineries all over Napa Valley. At Caymus there are two Cabernets: the Napa Valley bottling and Special Selection, which has been made most years since 1975 by selecting about a quarter of the best lots. Special Selection can come from any of the eight AVAs in which Caymus own or lease vineyards. It's usually 25% from mountain areas and 75% from the valley, but there's wide variation in sources depending on annual conditions. The style changed in the late nineties to become riper and richer, and since 2008 has included about 15% Merlot. Unlike some of the prominent Napa Valley Cabernets, Special Selection is made in good quantities, typically around 15,000 cases.

House style is definitely on the rich side. Caymus Napa Cabernet shows strong aromatic overtones of high-toned fruits, but when you go to Special Select, the aromatics become less obtrusive but the intensity on the palate deepens. Caymus is rich but Special Select is smoother and deeper. The Wagners also make Conundrum, which started as an entry-level white wine, blended from several varieties, sourced all over California; more recently a red has been added, made in a crowd-pleasing style that's very different from Caymus. There's also a Napa Valley Zinfandel.

Domaine Chandon Winery *

1 California Drive, Yountville, CA 94599
(1) 707 944 2892
customerservice@chandon.com
www.chandon.com
Yountville
Etoile
997 acres; 6,000,000 bottles
[map p. 49]

Moët & Chandon have expanded out of Champagne to establish subsidiaries in all corners of the globe. The first Chandon Estate was created in Argentina (1960), followed by Napa Valley (1973), Brazil (1973), Australia (1986), Nashik (India, 2013), and Ningxia (China, 2013). The Napa estate is located just outside of Yountville and was one of the first wineries in the area to make tourism a focus, with a tasting room and high-flying restaurant (now closed to make room for expanding the tasting room).

Chandon has 135 acres of vineyards around the winery, another vineyard on top of Mt. Veeder (overlooking the town of Napa) at 1,800 ft elevation, and 800 acres in Carneros. The focus is on the classic varieties of Champagne, Pinot Noir, Pinot Meunier, and Chardonnay. Initially there was basically a standard Brut and a special cuvée, Etoile, but now there are also rosé, Blanc de Noirs, Blanc de Blancs, single vineyard wines, and some limited editions. There is no vintage-dated wine in distribution, but small runs from individual years are available at the winery (together with some other small production wines). Still wines are about 10% of sales. The style is richer than Champagne, a little softer and plumper.

Chappellet Vineyard **

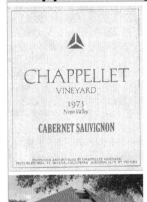

1581 Sage Canyon Road, St. Helena, CA 94574
(1) 707 286 4219
Philip Corallo-Titus
winery@chappellet.com
www.chappellet.com
St. Helena
Signature
$40
101 acres; 360,000 bottles
[map p. 49]

Chappellet is venerable as one of the first wineries to be built in Napa after Prohibition, in 1967 (one year after Mondavi). Driving up the narrow access road from Lake Hennessy, deep into the woods, it feels quite inaccessible. Vineyards aren't visible until you go around to the back of the pyramid-like winery. Covering 700 acres, the estate extends well beyond the vineyards, which range from 1000 to 1700 feet, just above the fog line. Grapes are also purchased from some neighboring vineyards. There were already vines on the property when it was purchased, but they were mostly Chenin Blanc. Following a replanting program in the nineties, most of the vineyard today is Cabernet Sauvignon.

There are two distinct Cabernet Sauvignons: Signature and Pritchard Hill. "The style has evolved but the goal has always been to make bold, fruity, wine. Signature was really designed to be ready; it has as much structure as any Cabernet to age, but we do try to reign in the tannins rather than have a heavy brooding style," says Ry Richards. "Pritchard Hill has a different stylistic objective: more extract, bigger tannins, pure black fruit, boysenberries, espresso coffee, a higher density overall." Signature, which uses 50% new oak, comes from the estate and east-facing hillsides in the vicinity; Pritchard Hill, with 100% new oak, is based on selection, and has been an estate wine from 2012. Both wines used to be 100% varietal but now are blends with just over 75% Cabernet Sauvignon; both also have Petit Verdot and Malbec, but there is Merlot only in Signature. There are 7,000 cases of Signature and 1,500 cases of Pritchard Hill. Beyond Cabernet, there's a full range of wines, mostly varietals.

Chase Family Cellars *

2252 Sulphur Springs Ave, St. Helena, CA 94574

(1) 707 963 1284

Alise Merritt

mail@chasecellars.com

www.chasecellars.com

St. Helena

St. Helena Zinfandel Reserve

$35

14 acres; 20,000 bottles

[map p. 50]

A residential street in St. Helena opens out at the end to reveal the Hayne vineyard, with Chase located in a house right at the edge. There is no sign, just a street number. The vineyard dates from 1872, and is now is divided into three parts owned by different members of the Hayne family. Chase has a 12 acre parcel of old Zinfandel, with vines up to 115 years old. Katie Hayne Simpson is the fifth generation owner. "Zin is the heart of Chase. For a family of this size to hold the old Zinfandel vines instead of planting high priced Cabernet Sauvignon is a passion play," she says.

Zinfandel is the core, but Chase also produces Petite Syrah from Calistoga and Cabernet Sauvignon from Stags Leap. The Hayne vineyard is dry farmed, and the vines are head pruned so there is essentially no canopy management. The side exposed to the morning sun is picked several days after the side exposed to afternoon sun (young vines—which means 35 years old—are harvested separately). The morning side has more energy and less alcohol and becomes the Reserve; the afternoon side becomes the Estate wine. The Estate Zinfandel is typical of the variety, with sweet high-toned aromatics, but the Reserve reaches a higher level. "This is the soul of Zin, you get the spice with the purity of fruits," says winemaker Russell Bevan. Its pure fruits are virtually unencumbered by tannins, but it does not go over the top, and is as close to elegance as Zinfandel gets.

The house style here shows refinement and purity; tannins aren't suppressed by powerful fruits but are so fine they recede into the background. This comes from what Russell calls aggressive winemaking. "Everything is pressed while still sweet and finishes fermentation in barrel. The switch is based on tasting tannins, when the wine has reached the level of phenolic extract we want, and there's sufficient flavor." Wines are intended to be consumed on release: "We're crafting wines that are approachable at young age, we give you wines that have verve and energy, so why not enjoy while they are young."

Colgin Cellars

**

220 Long Ranch Road, St. Helena, CA 94574

(1) 707 963 0999

Ann Colgin or Paul Roberts

info@colgincellars.com

www.colgincellars.com

St. Helena

IX Estate

34 acres; 40,000 bottles

[map p. 49]

One of the estates that created the cult wine movement, Colgin started with the 1992 vintage of Cabernet Sauvignon from the Herb Lamb vineyard (on the outskirts of Howell Mountain), when Helen Turley sourced the grapes from 14 rows in the most exposed position at the top. Herb Lamb continued to be a signature wine until the vineyard had to be replanted in 2008 (Colgin no longer makes it).

Two other wines come from vineyards around St. Helena. Ann Colgin purchased the Tychson Hill vineyard in 1995, and the first vintage was 2000; located at the north end of St. Helena, it was part of Freemark Abbey (but had collapsed during Prohibition and never been replanted). This is almost pure Cabernet Sauvignon. There's also the Cariad Bordeaux Blend, about half Cabernet Sauvignon, produced since 1999 from a blend between David Abreu's Madrona Ranch and Thorevilos vineyard.

The IX Estate on Pritchard Hill, where all wine is now made, was purchased in 1998; it takes its name from the fact that it was lot #9 on Long Ranch Road. It was planted with a traditional Bordeaux mix of varieties, with about two thirds Cabernet Sauvignon; the estate of 80 ha has 8 ha of vineyards, planted on east-facing slopes to catch the morning sun. The first vintage was 2002. In addition to the IX Estate Bordeaux blend, there's a small amount of Syrah. Focus is exclusively on high-end reds. Production of all wines is small: 1,200-1,500 cases of IX Estate, 250 cases of Tychson Hill, 500 cases of Cariad, and (previously) 500 cases of Herb Lamb.

Some change of style is evident over the years in the direction of greater refinement. Winemaker Allison Tauziet says any difference is due less to changes of vineyard source than to technical advances. "The biggest difference is the increased precision in viticulture. In the early years when we were making wine from Herb Lamb it was very rudimentary in the vineyard and vinification was in a custom crush," she points out. Current vintages are developing slowly: my concern is about the pace at which flavor variety will develop.

The Colgins sold a majority (60%) stake to luxury house LVMH in 2017—LVMH also own Domaine Chandon and Newton—but plan to stay on. Winemaking is not expected to change.

Corison Winery **

987 St. Helena Highway, St. Helena, CA 94574
(1) 707 963 0826
Cathy Corison
mail@corison.com
www.corison.com
St. Helena
Corison, Cabernet Sauvignon
Helios

14 acres; 30,000 bottles [map p. 50]

Cathy Corison has been fascinated with wine ever since she took a wine appreciation course in college; based on French wine, the course defined her reference point as European. She came to Napa in the early seventies and made wine at Chappellet through the eighties. She first made her own wine from purchased grapes, and continued to make wine for other producers until 2003.

The story behind the creation of her winery in Rutherford is that she was determined to find gravelly terroir for her Cabernet Sauvignon, and this turned up in the form of a neglected vineyard in Rutherford. There had been plans to develop the site but they had fallen through. This is the basis for her Kronos Cabernet Sauvignon, with vines (most likely clone 7) that were planted on St. George rootstock about forty years ago. Yields are punishingly low, as not only are the vines old, but the vineyard is infected with leaf roll virus. The extra concentration makes the Kronos Cabernet full and plush.

The Corison Cabernet Sauvignon is a monovarietal bottling, blended from three vineyards in the Rutherford-St. Helena area (some leased, one of which Cathy was recently able to purchase: "It's a big relief to secure the grapes and have complete control," she says). Corison Cabernet tends to come out around 14% alcohol, Kronos is usually closer to 13%. New oak is about 50%.

The latest cuvée is the Sunbasket Vineyard, first vintage 2014. Cathy has been purchasing grapes from the vineyard for 30 years, and recently was able to purchase it. Corison is also leasing four adjacent hectares and replanting them to Cabernet Sauvignon.

Graceful aging is a major stylistic objective. "Aging is very important to me. It's almost a moral imperative to make wines that will have a life," Cathy says. Indeed, the wines age slowly; at a vertical tasting in 2012, my favorite was the oldest in the tasting, the 2001. Since then the style seems to have become richer, as typified by the relatively powerful 2012, but a good acidic backbone keeps this in the tradition of ageworthy Cabernets. Production is about 400 cases of Kronos, and about 2,000 cases of Corison Cabernet. Beyond that, the winery has branched out to offer Cabernet Franc, a rosé from Cabernet Sauvignon, and a Gewürztraminer.

Diamond Creek Vineyards **

📍 1500 Diamond Mountain Road, Calistoga, CA 94515

📞 (1) 707 942 6926

Phil Ross

@ info@diamondcreekvineyards.com

🌐 www.diamondcreekvineyards.com

Diamond Mountain District

Gravelly Meadow, Cabernet Sauvignon

22 acres; 20,000 bottles

[map p. 49]

No one had planted vineyards this far north in the mountains when Al Brounstein purchased forested land on Diamond Mountain to create a vineyard in 1968, following a visit to the property with André Tchelistcheff and Louis Martini. Al was not happy with the quality of the Cabernet material that was available in California, but three of the first growths in Bordeaux sold him cuttings, which he then smuggled in by flying privately through Mexico. He was under pressure to plant on AxR1 but stuck to the St George rootstock because it had a good record in the mountains. He intended to emulate Bordeaux, and also planted Cabernet Franc, Merlot, and Malbec for the blend.

There are three individual vineyards, all with roughly the same blend of Cabernet Sauvignon, Merlot, and Cabernet Franc; Petit Verdot comes from a separate plot nearby. Gravelly Meadow is dry farmed, and the other vineyards have irrigation supplied by wells on the property, which has a small lake and a series of waterfalls. All the vineyards were planted at the same time, but Red Rock and Volcanic Hill started producing in 1972, whereas Gravelly Meadow did not produce until 1974. The oldest vines today date from 1988; Red Rock and Gravelly Meadow have more younger vines from a replanting program in the nineties. All vines have been propagated from the original selection, using a nursery on the property. A significant part of the difference between the vineyards is in the tannic structure—taut for Volcanic Hill, elegant for Red Rock, earthy for Gravelly Meadow—so will the characteristic differences between the wines narrow as the tannins resolve with age?

I tasted all three vineyards from 1994 to see whether the differences among current vintages were still evident after twenty years. With the moderate alcohol of the early nineties (12.5%), and delicately balanced palates, these were clearly all food wines, with some convergence in style compared to younger vintages. The fruit spectrum is similar in all three, just a touch more aromatic than you would find in

Bordeaux of the period, but there are differences in tannic structure. Volcanic Hill seemed the most mature, savory elements mingling with lightening fruits; Gravelly Meadow seemed the most precise and elegant, a tribute to the conventional wisdom that gravel goes with Cabernet; and Red Rock showed the most evident tannic structure. "Al thought Volcanic Hill would be the longest lived wine, but actually they all age equally well. But Volcanic always comes around last, there is no doubt about that," says Phil Ross. Production is small, around 500 cases each, except for only 100 cases of Lake when it is made. I could not say I have a favorite: in some vintages I prefer Volcanic Hill, and in others Gravelly Meadow. The winery remains committed to exclusively producing Cabernet blends.

Dominus Estate

**

2570 Napanook Rd, Yountville, CA 94599
(1) 707 944 8954
Tod Mostero
info@dominusestate.com
www.dominusestate.com
Yountville
Dominus
Napanook

123 acres; 100,000 bottles
[map p. 49]

While a graduate student in oenology at UC Davis, Christian Moueix worked the 1968 vineyard at Beaulieu in Rutherford. In 1982, as owner of Château Petrus in Pomerol, he entered into a partnership to produce wine from the part of the historic Napanook vineyard that was owned by John Daniel's daughter. Since then Moueix has been trying to reconstruct the vineyard in its entirety, and has almost succeeded—there's just a small strip at the top that is still owned by Domaine Chandon. The first release of Dominus, under the aegis of the John Daniel Society, was in 1983. In 1995, Christian Moueix became sole owner of the vineyard, and in 1996 the winery was constructed under the principle that it should blend invisibly into the landscape. It has an unusual double skin, with an outer construction of stones packed into netting hiding the construction inside—in the valley, it's sometimes called the stealth winery.

In 1996, Moueix introduced a second wine, called Napanook after the vineyard, which is produced by declassification. "At this point Dominus became more refined. But Napanook has experienced the same transition over the years towards greater refinement. Napanook is the same wine Dominus was ten years ago, we say among ourselves," says winemaker Tod Mostero. There's no discrimination between the lots up to the point when the wines go into barriques, with the best lots going into new wood; assemblage is nine months later, and Dominus typically gets 40% new oak and Napanook gets 20%. Grapes from a single plot may go into both wines, sometimes coming from opposite sides of the row (harvested separately); Napanook usually comes from the sunny side, Dominus comes from the more restrained shady side.

Dominus usually gives a polished, restrained, impression; it is one of the more restrained Cabernets in Napa. "Over-ripeness is the single most undesirable thing in Napa," says Christian Moueix. Some attitudes come straight from France. "We still make wine that is intended to be aged, you can probably start to drink five years after the harvest, but I consider that it doesn't really begin to become expressive until it's ten years, sometimes twenty," says Tod. Napanook is simpler, more approachable, more obvious. There are 6-7,000 cases of Dominus and 4-5,000 cases of Napanook.

The latest Moueix venture in Napa is Ulysses Vineyard, a property about a mile north of Dominus, purchased in 2008. It is a warmer spot than Dominus. Part of the old Hopper Ranch, the vineyard was being used by Swanson vineyards to produce their Merlot. Moueix replanted the vineyard to Cabernet Sauvignon, with a little Cabernet Franc and Petit Verdot. Made by the Dominus team, the first vintage was 2012.

Dunn Vineyards ★★

805 White Cottage Rd., Angwin, CA 9408
(1) 707 965 3642
Mike Dunn
ben@dunnvineyards.com
www.dunnvineyards.com
Howell Mountain
Howell Mountain, Cabernet Sauvignon
Napa Valley, Cabernet Sauvignon

41 acres; 54,000 bottles
[map p. 49]

One of the pioneers of Howell Mountain, Randy Dunn identified his vineyard in 1972 when he was winemaker at Caymus. Today it has expanded from the five original acres to about 34 acres planted in a much larger estate. The winery is a practical construction with some equipment outside, and the barrel room tunneled into the mountain. The original vineyard remains the core source for the Howell Mountain grapes, but is due for replanting soon, as yields have dropped significantly. Wine making is traditional; there's very little manipulation, no sorting of the grapes, stems are retained, and pump-overs are vigorous: "We do what we can to extract as much as possible," says Mike Dunn. The only exception is alcohol: Randy Dunn remains adamant that it must be less than 14%.

A program to eliminate Brett, in conjunction with a move to more new oak, lightened the style slightly in 2002. "Before 2002 the optimum age was more than twenty years: now?—give me ten years and we'll see," says Mike Dunn, adding, "I feel the need to repeat that the 'style' hasn't changed except for Brett management, barrel selection, and percent of new barrels." There are two Cabernet Sauvignons: Howell Mountain and Napa Valley. In fact, in a vertical tasting at the winery, my favorite was the Napa 1990. Production is around 3,000 cases of Howell Mountain and 1,200 cases of Napa Valley.

Since 2009, all the estate wine has gone into the Howell Mountain bottling. The Napa Valley bottling included wine from other sources on Howell Mountain as well as from elsewhere in the valley, but from 2009 to 2011 was all Howell Mountain, making it something of a second wine including declassified lots. Since 2012 the estate grapes have been supplemented by purchased grapes from two growers in Coombsville.

Eisele Vineyard Estate **

2155 Pickett Rd, Calistoga, CA

(1) 707 942 6061

Antoine Donnedieu de Vabres

wine@eiselevineyard.com

www.eiselevineyard.com

Calistoga

Eisele, Cabernet Sauvignon

② Altagracia

37 acres; 50,000 bottles

[map p. 49]

At the northern end of the valley, within a protected canyon east of Calistoga, the Eisele Vineyard has a distinguished history. It was first planted as a vineyard in 1886; Cabernet Sauvignon was planted in 1964. The vineyard is named for the Eisele's, who owned it in the 1970s and 1980s. Paul Draper of Ridge Vineyards made the first commercial release in 1971; this was the one and only vintage of Ridge Eisele. In 1972 and 1973 the grapes were sold to Mondavi (reportedly for the Reserve Cabernet Sauvignon). In 1974, Conn Creek Winery produced the second vineyard-labeled release, and then from 1975 the grapes were sold to Joseph Phelps, who produced a vineyard-designated wine until 1991.

After the property was purchased by Bart and Daphne Araujo in 1991, they made the wine at the estate under the Araujo label. It's difficult to compare the Cabernet from Eisele before and after 1991 given vintage variation and differences in age, but it's interesting that in the one year that both Phelps and Araujo released an Eisele bottling, the wines today show more similarities than differences. The Araujo shows more complex, attractive fruits and is more open; the style of the Phelps is more reserved (in line with earlier Eisele vintages and with their Insignia blend of the period). A savory aromatic thread, somewhat reminiscent of the French garrigue, runs through both wines, giving an impression that the vineyard is expressing its terroir.

The vineyard was heavily virused so the Araujos started an extensive replanting program, but the virusing prevented using selection massale. However, some years earlier, Shafer's home vineyard had been planted with cuttings from Eisele, and Shafer returned the favor with cuttings that were propagated to make the "young" Eisele selection. Cuttings from Eisele were later cured of viruses, and became the "old" Eisele selection. After twenty years, the original vines are now being replanted.

Eisele has an unusual terroir. The vineyards are on an alluvial fan coming straight off the Palisades mountains, but they are not very fertile, and fertility decreases going away from the mountain. Going up the slope you get more clay soils and higher vigor, the opposite of the usual order. The property has 70 ha, and 15 ha are planted out of 16 plantable hectares. Cabernet Sauvignon is planted in the most gravelly part of the vineyard, but there are blocks of Merlot, Petit Verdot, Cabernet Franc, Syrah, Sauvignon Blanc, and Viognier. In the early days, the Phelps Eisele was 100% Cabernet Sauvignon, as were the first two Araujo vintages, but since then the wine has been a blend, usually 85-95% Cabernet Sauvignon with some Cabernet Franc and Petit Verdot, sometimes also a little Merlot. Since 1999 there has been a second wine, Altagracia, also based on a Bordeaux blend, but which fluctuates more widely in varietal composition, from 58% to 100% Cabernet Sauvignon.

In 2013, the estate was sold to François Pinault of Château Latour; in 2016 he changed the name from Araujo Estate to Eisele Vineyard Estate. The Araujos started a new venture called Accendo Cellars (see mini-profile), the year after selling the Araujo Estate.

Far Niente *

 1350 Acacia Dr, Oakville, CA 94562

(1) 707 944 2861

Nicole Marchesi

info@farniente.com

www.farniente.com

Oakville

Martin Stelling Vineyard, Cabernet Sauvignon

Oakville Cabernet Sauvignon

Napa Chardonnay

274 acres; 500,000 bottles

[map p. 50]

Just across from Martha's Vineyard, Far Niente is an gothic building dating from the mid nineteenth century. Approached by a long, elegant drive, it's surrounded by gardens rather than vineyards. An old property that had fallen into disrepair, it was purchased by Gil and Beth Nickel in 1979. The old stone house was restored; for the first three years wine was made offsite, but in 1982 resumed at the property. The caves underneath the building where the barriques are stored were constructed recently, in stages since 1990. Then in 1997 the Nickels purchased the Sullenger property, also in Oakville, which they renamed as Nickel & Nickel, which focuses on a series of single vineyard wines. (Some fruit from the John C. Sullenger vineyard goes into Far Niente Napa Cabernet.) A majority stake in both properties was sold to GI Partners, a San Francisco private equity firm, in 2016.

Far Niente focuses on two varietal wines: Chardonnay and Cabernet Sauvignon. "The model is to make one truly great Chardonnay and Cabernet in each vintage," says winemaker Nicole Marchesi. The major source for estate grapes is the Martin Stelling Vineyard, named for a former owner who built up the vineyard, but died before it produced grapes. Located just to the west of the winery, running up to the hills of Oakville, it was planted in 1978 with Cabernet Sauvignon and other Bordeaux varieties. Far Niente has been 100% Oakville since 2001 (production declined when the other sources ceased to be used). The Cabernet Sauvignon is smooth and approachable, with a silky texture. I remember when the Chardonnay used to show a powerful oaky style, but today it is sourced largely from Coombsville and the style is leaner.

Another single vineyard Cabernet will be introduced as the result of the purchase of a 60 acre parcel in Rutherford in 2017. Far Niente also owns Dolce, a property in Coombsville that produces a late harvest wine from a vineyard farmed to encourage botrytis. A blend of Sémillon with Sauvignon Blanc, Dolce is one of Napa's few dessert wines.

Grgich Hills Estate

1829 St. Helena Highway, Rutherford, CA 94573

(1) 800 532 3057

Ivo Jeramaz

info@grgich.com

www.grgich.com

Rutherford

Rutherford Cabernet Sauvignon

Carneros Chardonnay

$20

365 acres; 780,000 bottles

[map p. 50]

An immigrant from Croatia who arrived in America with nothing but a small suitcase, Mike Grgich was at Beaulieu during the 1960s, and then gained instant fame as the winemaker who crafted the 1973 Chardonnay at Chateau Montelena that won the Judgment of Paris tasting in 1976. Together with a business partner in 1977, he founded his own winery, Grgich Hills, in Rutherford. His nephew Ivo Jeramaz came from Croatia to help, and today Ivo's daughter is involved, so the estate is into the third generation (which however seems short compared to the 15 generations of winemakers back in Croatia).

The estate has an extensive range of vineyards in five locations, all the way from south to north in Napa, in Carneros, American Canyon, Yountville, Rutherford, and Calistoga. "Mike was very smart," says Ivo, "he bought land early and never paid more than $20,000 an acre." The property changed its name to Grgich Hills Estate in 2003 to reflect the fact that since then only estate grapes have been used. "Production went down 40% but we are very happy that we are making better wines," Ivo adds. All vineyards are dry farmed, and farming is intensely organic (in fact basically biodynamic), with a range of birds to eat the insects, and several acres of flower and other plants with bees kept, to avoid the problems of monoculture.

Although Chardonnay was where Mike made his reputation, it is no longer the main focus. "Napa is not known for great Chardonnay any more—there is Chardonnay made everywhere—but Napa has a monopoly on great Cabernet. We used to make more Chardonnay than Cabernet but now it's reversed," Ivo explains. Still there is a hierarchy of Chardonnays: "Napa is the village wine, Carneros (from a single vineyard) is premier cru, and then there is Miljenko's Selection from specific vineyard blocks." The Carneros, perhaps because it has no new oak and malolactic fermentation is blocked, is the most elegant; it ages well for a decade. There are Cabernets from Napa, Rutherford, and Yountville, all moderate in style, but my favorite is Rutherford for its slight aromatic lift. The house style is never over stated.

Groth Vineyards & Winery *

750 Oakville Crossroad, Oakville, CA 94562
(1) 707 944 0290
Suzanne Groth
info@grothwines.com
www.grothwines.com
Oakville
Oakville Cabernet Sauvignon
Napa Valley, Hillview Vineyard Chardonnay
$35
160 acres; 860,000 bottles [map p. 50]

Groth is a classic story of a family who moved from elsewhere to start and run a winery in Napa. Dennis and Judy Groth came from computer maker Atari and bought a contiguous block of 120 acres on the valley floor in Oakville in 1981, followed by a smaller property south of Yountville. Production began immediately and increased rapidly, and by 1985 the winery was a full time occupation. The striking pink building (intended to follow the style of the old Missions) was constructed in 1990 and extended in 2007. Michael Weis, now winemaker emeritus, was in charge for twenty years until he handed over to Cameron Parry in 2014.

The Oakville property is planted with Cabernet Sauvignon and Sauvignon Blanc; Merlot and Chardonnay are planted at Yountville. Sauvignon Blanc is the largest production, just ahead of Cabernet Sauvignon: Chardonnay is only about 10%. Groth makes only four wines: the three varietals plus a Cabernet Reserve. The Oakville Cabernet includes grapes from other growers in Oakville, but the Reserve comes only from a specific 27 acre block in the northwest corner of the estate, with soils of sedimentary rocks. "In terms of Oakville, remember that soils vary from clay to alluvial to loess. So the Reserve is a wine of one place, but the Oakville Cabernet is a reflection of everything that is happening in Oakville," says Michael Weis. Although it includes some Merlot, the style emphasizes purity of fruits to give an impression of the penetrating linearity of pure Cabernet Sauvignon. The Reserve is more intense, spicy and chocolaty.

"The Chardonnay comes from the Hillside Vineyard south of Yountville because that region is 15% cooler. Chardonnay from here is not as vibrant as from Yountville. Groth has always made a non-malo Chardonnay, that's the style of the house. Malo adds a dimension to the wine that I don't like, I'd rather have something clean and crisper," Michael says. The Sauvignon Blanc (all from the Oakville estate and local growers, although it is labeled as Napa Valley) is fermented in old barrels and shows a rich style, with exotic fruit notes. The wines offer a good representation of the current character of Napa Valley.

HALL

*

401 St. Helena Highway S, St. Helena, CA 94574
(1) 707 967 2626
Steve Leveque
visit@hallwines.com
www.hallwines.com
Rutherford
Napa, Kathryn Hall Cabernet Sauvignon
$40
1,200,000 bottles
[map p. 50]

The winery in St. Helena stands on a site where wine has been made since 1885; at one time it became a cooperative, and Kathryn Hall purchased it in 2002. Designed for Cabernet production, the glass-sided post-modern winery has fermentation tanks visible through the glass. HALL produces around ten different Cabernet Sauvignons, extending from the Napa Cabernet Sauvignon, which includes a little Merlot and is about a third of production, to wines from individual AVAs or single vineyards. "We source grapes from top vineyards in thirteen of the Napa AVAs," says winemaker Megan Gunderson Paredes, "with about 40% coming from estate vineyards."

There is a focus on vineyard designates, which are generally 100% Cabernet Sauvignon, although there are also wines designed to show the art of blending (more between sources than between varieties). The approachable Napa North End Cabernet is intended to show the juiciness of fruit from the valley north of St. Helena. By contrast, Ellie's Cabernet comes from mountain fruit and is taut and more restrained. New oak is around 75% for the blended wines, and increases to 90% for the single vineyard wines, which tend to be sterner and to require a few years before drinking.

House style shows an underlying sweetness and refined texture from both valley floor and mountain, but alcohol levels are high, often around or above 15%. "These wines are delicious expressions of their sites, I don't want to put on parameters that will limit them," Megan says. The style is smooth, you might say sleek rather than unctuous. The WALT program, introduced in 2010 to focus on Pinot Noir and Chardonnay, sources grapes from Anderson Valley and Santa Rita Hills as well as Carneros and Sonoma. Another winery is being built at Sebastopol for it. Only ten of the larger production HALL or WALT wines are available in general distribution.

In addition to the facility in St. Helena, where it's possible to walk in, there is also tasting room in Rutherford, requiring appointments, and focusing specifically on the limited-production wines.

Harlan Estate ***

📍 1567 Oakville Grade, Oakville, CA 94562
📞 (1) 707 944 1441
Summer Jimenez
@ info@harlanestate.com
🌐 www.harlanestate.com
Oakville
Harlan Estate
② The Maiden
39 acres; 32,000 bottles
[map p. 50]

Harlan's two hundred acre estate is a beautiful property in the hills above Oakville, overlooking Martha's Vineyard, To Kalon, and Napanook. After several years searching for land in Napa, Bill Harlan bought the land in tranches, starting in 1984, and planted the vineyards between 1985 and the early 1990s. The estate rises from 200 feet to 1,000 feet, with the vineyards planted up to 500 feet. The original vineyards were planted at 1,800 vines/ha, which was considered a relatively high density at the time, but subsequent plantings have moved up to 5,400 vines/ha, and even 7,500 (positively Bordeaux-like).

The plantings are a classic Médoc mix, about 70% Cabernet Sauvignon, the rest Merlot, Cabernet Franc, and Petit Verdot. About three quarters of the terroir is volcanic, and one quarter sedimentary; Merlot is grown on the sedimentary soils as they have better water retention.

None of the first three vintages (1987-1989) were sold commercially; the first commercial vintage, 1990, was released in 1996. Michel Rolland is the consulting winemaker. A second wine, The Maiden, is about a quarter of production. The wines age well: recently my favorite vintage has oscillated between the 1991 and the 1995.

Together with winemaker Bob Levy, Bill Harlan started a second operation in 1997; BOND has the same winemaking team, but here the objective is to produce cuvées that express different terroirs, with individual vineyards ranging from 7 to 11 acres in a variety of locations on both sides of the valley. At last count there were five cuvées. I find the style of the BOND cuvées to be noticeably richer and more obviously New World in origin than that of Harlan. Bill Harlan's latest project is Promontory (see mini-profile), a new winery in the foothills of Mount Veeder.

Heitz Cellars *

436 St. Helena Highway, St. Helena, CA 94574

(1) 707 963 3542

Tiffany Egan

info@heitzcellar.com

www.heitzcellar.com

St. Helena

Trailside Vineyard, Cabernet Sauvignon

424 acres; 480,000 bottles

[map p. 50]

Dating from the 1960s, Heitz is now regarded as one of the venerable old Napa producers. Joe Heitz started as André Tchelistcheff's assistant at Beaulieu in 1951, spent a period running the Department of Enology at Fresno State University, and then returned to the valley to launch Heitz with 8 acres of land along route 29. The original winery is the site of the Heitz tasting room today. The present winery in St. Helena was purchased in 1964, and about 50 acres of vineyards were planted around it. However, the real breakthrough came in 1965 when the Heitz's started buying Cabernet Sauvignon grapes from Tom and Martha May's vineyard in Oakville. Initially the grapes were blended into the general Cabernet bottling, but then Joe decided to make a single vineyard wine (the first in California). From its first vintage in 1966, Heitz Martha's Vineyard was regarded as a benchmark for Napa Cabernet; the 1974 is still regarded as one of the best wines ever made in California. It was made by Joe's son, David, who is still the winemaker today.

Heitz has always produced an extensive line of varietals, including the Napa Valley Cabernet, Zinfandel, Chardonnay, and Sauvignon Blanc, but none has achieved the acclaim of the single vineyard Cabernets. After the initial years, Cabernet Sauvignon grapes were purchased to augment the supply for the Napa Valley Cabernet, but today the only grapes not coming from the estate itself are those from Martha's Vineyard. In fact, having purchased the 217 acre Ink Grade Vineyard just east of Howell Mountain, Heitz has surplus grapes to sell. The latest acquisition is the Linda Falls Vineyard on Howell Mountain, comprising 10 acres of Cabernet Sauvignon.

In addition to its most famous wine, there have been two other single vineyard Cabernets, Bella Oaks (in Rutherford) and Trailside (on the other side of the valley by the Silverado Trail). Like Martha's Vineyard, Bella Oaks belonged to a couple, Barney and Belle Rhodes, who sold the entire crop to Heitz. Production of Bella Oaks stopped in 2007, because the vineyard was sold. The style with the single vineyard Cabernets is for quite extended oak aging, with one year in old foudres of American oak followed by thirty months in French barriques, including a high proportion of new oak (usually 60% for Bella Oaks, 70-80% for Martha's Vineyard and 100% for Trailside). Certainly there is a similarity of style, especially between Bella Oaks and Martha's Vineyard, although Martha's Vineyard is always the most intense, and needs the most time to come around. I still don't think any subsequent vintage has equaled the 1974.

An infection in the winery with TCA made the vintages from 1985 questionable (the 1987 was the worst affected), and it took several years for the problem to be recognized; the wines did not become completely free of cork taint until 1992. And then the vineyard had to be replanted because of phylloxera, so there was no vintage in 1995; the wine came from relatively young vines for the rest of the decade. Has Martha's Vineyard ever fully recovered its reputation? Some recent vintages suggest a road to recovery; others seem to have lost their way.

For all the ups and downs, Heitz remains an icon in Napa Valley, but was sold in 2018 to Galyon Lawrence, from a family involved in agriculture and industry.

Inglenook

1991 St Helena Highway, Rutherford, CA 94573
(1) 707 968 1100
reservations@inglenook.com
www.inglenook.com
Rutherford
Rubicon, Cabernet Sauvignon
$45
326 acres; 3,200,000 bottles
[map p. 50]

The old Inglenook winery at the heart of Rutherford has a chequered history. Some people regard it as the birthplace of fine wine, or at least of fine wine based on Cabernet Sauvignon, in Napa. Finnish sea captain Gustave Niebaum, who made a fortune trading furs in Alaska, decided after a visit to France that the gravelly loam soils of Rutherford resembled Bordeaux and might reward attempts to produce the same blend of wine. He planted Cabernet Sauvignon, together with Cabernet Franc and Merlot. A splendid Gothic mansion was constructed to house winemaking.

Inglenook Cabernets were famous in the period after Prohibition. The winery was sold to United Vintners in 1964, and then became part of Heublein when United Vintners was itself sold in 1969. Quality went out of the window. In 1975, film director Francis Ford Coppola purchased Niebaum's former home together with 49 hectares of surrounding vineyards, and then in 1995 Heublein tired of the business and sold him the Inglenook winery and the rest of the vineyards. The house is now a visitor center, and viticulture and vinification have been modernized. The original holdings were reunited under the name Rubicon Estate. The Inglenook name was sold to Constellation, who sold it to The Wine Group in 2008; it was used for jug wine until Coppola got it back in 2011.

The winery is now called Inglenook, and the top wine is called Rubicon (a classic blend with about 86% Cabernet Sauvignon). The second wine was previously called CASK, but now is labeled simply as Inglenook Cabernet Sauvignon (it's a similar blend to Rubicon). The wines are quite mainstream for Napa. There's also Syrah, Zinfandel, Sauvignon Blanc, and a Rhône-style white. Francis Coppola also has two wineries in Sonoma, and production of most of the wines under the Inglenook label has been moved to the Francis Ford Coppola Winery. Rubicon is only 60,000 bottles out of the total.

Jarvis Winery   *

2970 Monticello Rd, Napa, CA 94558
(1) 800 255 5280
William Jarvis
wines@jarvisnapa.com
www.jarviswines.com
Napa Valley
Cabernet Sauvignon Reserve
$80
37 acres; 85,000 bottles
[map p. 49]

The creation of William Jarvis, whose career was in Silicon Valley, Jarvis has a rather unusual facility, a bunker cut into the mountain (using the equipment that created the Channel tunnel between England and France). The tunnel curves around in a large circle, with rooms off to the side and tanks and vats along the way.

Well to the east of Napa Valley proper, vineyards are at 1,000 foot elevation and are around 6 degrees cooler than the valley floor. There are several separate vineyards occupying 37 planted acres out of a total estate of 1,320 acres. Fermentation is all in stainless steel, with some rotary tanks used for Cabernet Sauvignon and Cabernet Franc. MLF is performed in large wooden vats, then the wine goes into barrels. Production is only estate wine; the first vintage was 1992.

The focus is on Cabernet Sauvignon, using one of the clones that performed best in the trials at Beaulieu, giving low yields. Most of the wines are single varietals, particularly Cabernet Sauvignon, Cabernet Franc, Merlot, and Chardonnay. The Reserve designation is used for the top wines, which are barrel selections. The Lake William cuvée was created by accident when William Jarvis pumped Cabernet Franc into a tank of Cabernet Sauvignon. Consulting winemaker Dimitri Tchelistcheff was very cross, until it turned out that the wine was actually rather successful, and it has now become a regular bottling in the range. The Cabernet Sauvignon has quite a restrained style, the Reserve has more density and chocolate notes, the Lake William actually seems more tightly structured, and the top Chardonnay, Finch Hollow, tends towards the exotic.

Joseph Phelps Vineyards **

200 Taplin Road, St. Helena, CA 94574

(1) 800 707 5789

Bill Phelps

preferred@josephphelps.com

www.josephphelps.com

St. Helena

Napa Valley, Cabernet Sauvignon

St. Helena, Sauvignon Blanc

$75

474 acres; 780,000 bottles

[map p. 50]

Phelps is one of the most reliable producers in Napa. It has expanded significantly, with vineyards in Sonoma as well as various locations in Napa Valley, and Pinot Noir, Sauvignon Blanc, and Viognier also in its line up, but the heart of the operation remains in Cabernet Sauvignon. Its most famous wine is Insignia.

Insignia is one of California's most genuine cult wines, meaning that it is produced in appreciable quantities (up to 20,000 cases), roughly comparable to a Bordeaux château. As a selection of the best cuvées, it should represent the best of the vintage, but at these quantities should still be strongly influenced by general vintage character. It has been a Cabernet-dominated blend since the 1980s, averaging around 80% Cabernet Sauvignon, with the remainder coming from all the other Bordeaux varieties in varying proportions. The grapes originate in about six vineyard plots, in various parts of Napa Valley. Vintage 2003 was the last year in which any grapes came from growers: today the wine is entirely an estate production.

The wine is not easy to judge when young, given the powerful fruits, which take ten years or more, depending on vintage, to resolve enough to allow complexity to show. I am inclined to divide the Insignias into two series. There's a lineage of vintages 1997, 2001, 2007, which seems more European in balance and restraint; there's an alternative lineage from 1999, 2002, 2008, which shows more overt fruit and aromatics in the New World style. I could not see any direct correlation with varietal composition, which changes in order to maintain consistency of style, and it therefore seems that the differences reflect vintage character, which is as it should be.

Kongsgaard Wine **

4375 Atlas Peak Road, Napa, CA 94558

(1) 707 226 2190

John Kongsgaard

info@kongsgaardwine.com

www.kongsgaardwine.com

Atlas Peak

Napa Chardonnay

24 acres; 36,000 bottles

[map p. 49]

Standing in the winery, a cave tunneled into the mountain, Alex Kongsgaard says, "You're looking at the whole business here, Mom and Dad (John and Maggie Kongsgaard) and the two of us" (Alex and vineyard manager Evan Frazier). Kongsgaard is certainly a small producer. Located just short of the end of the road at the summit of Atlas Peak, at an elevation of 2,200 feet, it is not the most accessible vineyard. The winery is nothing if not discrete, and it's easy to shoot past and end up at the Kongsgaard's residence. The location is a bit off the beaten track from the rest of Atlas Peak, as most vineyards are located on Soda Canyon Road, running parallel on the slopes of the mountain just to the north. John Kongsgaard was winemaker at Newton for fifteen years, and then spent a period at Luna, where he also made his own wines, before moving to Atlas Peak in 2006.

Kongsgaard is most famous for its Chardonnay, The Judge, which comes from a small (5 acre) vineyard on an outcrop between Napa and Coombsville. That property has been in the family for almost a hundred years. "It's basically a rock pile, it was explicitly purchased as a rock pile by my great grandfather who was going to quarry it," Alex explains. That never happened, but a few houses were built, and John Kongsgaard ended up planting a vineyard in what was basically his backyard. "It's a very extreme site. The soil is so poor that if we take a sample to the soil science people, they say it's not possible to grow anything," Alex says. Before John Kongsgaard started bottling it separately, the grapes were sold to Newton and were part of the Unfiltered Chardonnay. Even though the site is small, there's significant variation in the soil, and barrel samples show variation from sweet, ripe citrus-driven, flavors, picked early and put into natural oak, to richer more stone fruits put into new oak. Fermentation is very slow: in February 2017 some lots from the 2016 vintage still had not finished fermentation. It's a powerful, full-flavored wine, but has what would be a sense of tannic restraint if it were a red wine. Alcohol is around 15%: "to us that's the level the wine achieves at the peak of ripeness and flavor development," Alex says. "The Judge pushes towards mineral, but the Napa Chardonnay is more openly expressive, more easily approachable."

The Napa Chardonnay is the flagship wine, the only one in national distribution, mostly sourced from the Hyde and Hudson vineyards in Carneros, although like all the Kongsgaard wines it is labeled as Napa AVA. "John generally takes a dim view of the AVA system as not really being useful to us," Alex explains. The Cabernet has a touch of Merlot in most years; originally grapes came from Abreu, but now come from the home vineyard, which was planted in 2009 and came on line in 2014, and from neighboring vineyards. Other cuvées include a Merlot, the Fimasaurus Merlot-Cabernet blend, and Syrah, but all in very small amounts. The reds are rich and chocolaty, with the Cabernet very pure and deep, Fimasaurus broader, Merlot offering a more uplifted impression, and Syrah nutty and elegant. The wines go on sale in August each year and typically sell out to the mailing list in a few weeks. Then there is no more until the next release.

Larkmead Vineyards *

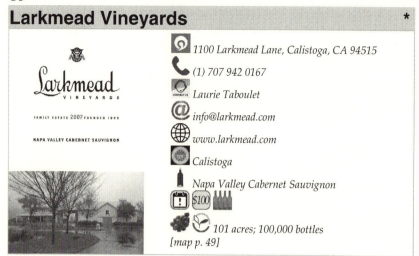

1100 Larkmead Lane, Calistoga, CA 94515
(1) 707 942 0167
Laurie Taboulet
info@larkmead.com
www.larkmead.com
Calistoga
Napa Valley Cabernet Sauvignon
$100
101 acres; 100,000 bottles
[map p. 49]

One of the oldest wineries in Napa, Larkmead was established in 1873. It was one of the Big Four after Repeal, but the modern era starts from 1987 when production restarted, using a custom crush facility until the new winery was built in 2005. The vineyards are around the winery, right at the northern end of Napa Valley where the Mayacamas and Vaca mountain ranges all but join together. It is a very hot spot in summer. The original winery is a stone house across the street from the modern buildings, where the tasting room is housed in a charming white building; the winery, a practical building with a vat room and two barrel rooms, is just behind.

The focus is on red wine, with a small production of Sauvignon Blanc and Tocai Friulano (actually the oldest vines on the property). The basic red comes from the youngest vines, with the blend depending on the year. The White Label wines are blends that are released in the Spring, and include Firebelle (a Merlot-based blend), Cabernet Sauvignon (the workhorse wine), Lillie (Sauvignon Blanc blend), and LMV Salon (Cabernet Franc blend). The Black Label wines are released later, in the Fall, and come from single plots. Aside from the Tocai, they are all varietal Cabernet Sauvignon, including Dr. Olmo (from a plot of gravel), Solari (from a mix of gravel and clay), and The Lark (from an atypical sandy plot).

The house style is fine and silky, from Firebelle with its slightly higher-toned aromatics, to the smoky Napa Cabernet, the tight Dr. Olmo, and the nutty Solari. The intention is that wines can be enjoyed immediately on release, and certainly the tannins are fine enough not to present an obstacle, but flavor variety is better developed if you wait three or four years after release.

Louis Martini Winery

254 St. Helena Highway South, St. Helena, CA 94574

(1) 707 963 2736

info@louismartini.com

www.louismartini.com

St. Helena

Monte Rosso, Zinfandel

$25

1,200,000 bottles

[map p. 50]

One of the oldest established wine producers in California, Louis Martini had its origins when the first Louis started making wine at the beginning of the twentieth century, and somewhat unusually formed his own company during Prohibition to produce sacramental wine and kits for home winemaking. At the end of Prohibition he built a winery in St. Helena. In 1938 he expanded into Sonoma by purchasing the Goldstein Ranch (originally planted in the 1880s), which he renamed Monte Rosso. In 1951 his son, also Louis Martini, took over winemaking, and in 1977 the third generation, Michael Martini, took over. The winery and vineyards were sold to Gallo in 2002. Martini's general production is more or less standard for Napa, but Monte Rosso really is a special representation of Sonoma.

The best known vineyard in Sonoma, Monte Rosso is renowned for both its old Zinfandel and Cabernet Sauvignon. Today there are 25 ha of Zinfandel, 40 ha of Cabernet Sauvignon, and 6 ha of Petite Syrah or other varieties. There are two blocks of white grapes. Martini produces several wines from Monte Rosso. The most famous is probably the gnarly vine Zinfandel, which comes from some of the oldest plantings, followed by the (100%) Cabernet Sauvignon. A special blend called Los Ninos was produced from 1979, initially as a Cabernet, then becoming a Meritage after 1985; the blend included Petit Verdot for the first few years and from 2001 had Cabernet Franc as the other variety. In 2008 Martini introduced a Proprietary Red, which is more than half Petit Verdot with one third Cabernet Sauvignon.

Mayacamas Vineyards *

1155 Lokoya Road, Napa CA 94558

(1) 707 224 4030

Jimmy Hayes

contact@mayacamas.com

www.mayacamas.com

Mount Veeder

Mt. Veeder Cabernet Sauvignon

Mt. Veeder Chardonnay

51 acres; 90,000 bottles [map p. 49]

"The road from St. Helena is closed by a mud slide, be sure to come from Oakville," I was warned before I set out for Mayacamas. It may be only 20 minutes from downtown Napa, but driving up the narrow, winding, precipitous road onto Mount Veeder, it feels quite inaccessible, which is all the more surprising as it is one of the older wineries, dating from the nineteenth century. The estate is well up in the mountains at the border of Napa and Sonoma, with vineyards at elevations from 1,800 to 2,400 feet, and views across to San Pablo Bay. The only way to see the vineyards is in an open off-road vehicle; driving through the extended forest, you come to clearings with vineyards. There are 25 individual vineyard plots, at varying elevations and exposures. Soils are varied but generally volcanic; there is extreme diurnal variation.

The modern history of the estate dates from the ownership of Bob Travers, who built up the property from 1968 and made some famous Cabernet Sauvignons in the seventies. But the property became run down in recent years, and by the time it was sold in 2013, most wine came from grapes purchased from growers on Mount Veeder. After some problems between the new partners, the Schottenstein family took 100% ownership in 2016. They are replanting 85% of the vineyards, but believe it will be a fifteen year process before Mayacamas returns completely to estate production. "Bob Travers made a huge variety of wines, but we are confining the focus to Cabernet Sauvignon, Merlot, and Chardonnay," says sales manager Artie Johnson.

The intention is to keep the style of Mayacamas: "We are replanting with heritage clones because we don't want to change the style in the glass." For Chardonnay, this is relatively lean, with minimal exposure to new oak and malolactic fermentation blocked. "The wine tends to start very simple and closed down, and then it begins to develop around the time of release," explains winemaker Braiden Albrecht. It takes another year for flavor variety to develop. Current releases of the Cabernet show increased purity from the old style, with a sense of the precision of the black fruits reinforced by the volcanic mountain soils. While this is very much a work in progress, there is good potential for Mayacamas to define the classic character of mountain Cabernet.

Chateau Montelena ★★

 1429 Tubbs Lane, Calistoga, CA 94515

 (1) 707 942 5105

 Jeff Adams

 reservations@montelena.com

 www.montelena.com

 Calistoga

Cabernet Sauvignon, Montelena Estate

Napa Valley, Chardonnay

 Napa Valley, Cabernet Sauvignon

 $30

 247 acres; 400,000 bottles

[map p. 49]

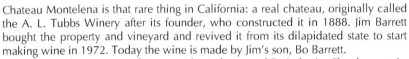

Chateau Montelena is that rare thing in California: a real chateau, originally called the A. L. Tubbs Winery after its founder, who constructed it in 1888. Jim Barrett bought the property and vineyard and revived it from its dilapidated state to start making wine in 1972. Today the wine is made by Jim's son, Bo Barrett.

Although Chateau Montelena won the Judgment of Paris for its Chardonnay, its Cabernet Sauvignon was one of the trendsetters through the 1970s. This has now become the Montelena Estate bottling, sourced from the vineyards around the winery at the very northern limit of Napa Valley. The elevation is around 400 foot, which no doubt compensates for the increase in temperature that's usually found going up the valley. The wine is a blend from several sites that ripen over a 4-6 week period, increasing complexity. It has a long and distinguished reputation for elegance.

But there is also another, completely different, Cabernet Sauvignon, also under the Napa Valley appellation, which comes from other vineyards and is made in a much simpler style. The only distinction between them on the bottle is a gold band stating "The Montelena Estate" on the original bottling. It would be easy to become confused. Personally, I like the older vintages better than the more powerful recent vintages; the 1985 was still going strong in 2012. Neither the white nor red shows New World exuberance; the style is relatively restrained, but there's a tendency in more recent vintages for the wines to tighten up and become leaner, losing that flush of youthful fruit that makes them so attractive.

Morlet Family Vineyards ★★

2825 St. Helena Highway North, St. Helena, CA 94574
(1) 707 967 8690
Luc & Jodie Morlet
info@morletwines.com
www.morletwines.com
St. Helena
Sonoma Coast, Joli Coeur Pinot Noir
Napa, Passionément Cabernet Sauvignon
Sonoma County, Ma Douce Chardonnay
$150   69 acres; 72,000 bottles [map p. 50]

"I don't see myself as a traditionalist, we define our winemaking as neoclassical, neo for the New World and classical because we represent a thousand years of winemaking (in France)," says Luc Morlet. The restored mansion that is Morlet's headquarters is just behind St. Helena, looking out towards the Vaca mountains. The atmosphere feels more residential than commercial. Luc comes from Champagne, and visits start with a glass of champagne from the family domaine, Pierre Morlet.

Luc started in Napa by making wine at Newton and Peter Michael, and began producing his own wine in 2006. He has been accumulating vineyards, with a couple of acres around the house, a small parcel in Knights Valley, and most recently an abandoned vineyard on the Oakville Bench. Production will be three quarters based on estate grapes, split more or less equally between Napa and Sonoma, although moving more towards Napa as the estate vineyards come on line. Cabernet Sauvignons come from Napa, while Pinot Noir and Chardonnay come from Sonoma. In each case, there are cuvées from specific vineyards and blends from different sources. "All the wines are terroir-driven, but as a Champenoise I believe in assemblage. Chardonnays Ma Douce and Ma Princesse are exclusively about terroir, but Coup de Coeur is a barrel selection of the best lots."

Almost all the great French varieties are made here. The varietal Passionément shows the direct purity of Cabernet Sauvignon fruits, the Mon Chevalier blend shows typically more breadth. The Syrah (Bouquet Garni) resembles the Northern Rhône aromatically but shows the fullness of the New World on the palate. The Pinot Noirs are characteristically earthy, sweet, and ripe. Chardonnays are in the New World tradition, full bodied and rich, but with a flavor spectrum that brings Burgundy to mind. There is even a Sémillon-Sauvignon Blanc blend (La Proportion Dorée) intended to resemble Pessac-Léognan. All the wines have French names, and Luc is busy recapitulating the aromas and flavors of his native France, although the wines have the richer, full-bodied quality of the New World.

Newton Vineyard   **

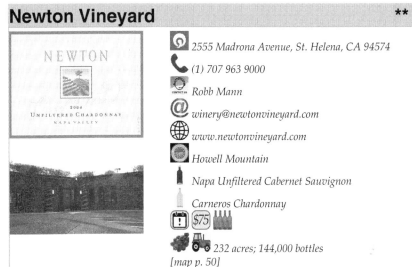

2555 Madrona Avenue, St. Helena, CA 94574
(1) 707 963 9000
Robb Mann
winery@newtonvineyard.com
www.newtonvineyard.com
Howell Mountain
Napa Unfiltered Cabernet Sauvignon
Carneros Chardonnay
$75
232 acres; 144,000 bottles
[map p. 50]

After founding Sterling Vineyards in Calistoga in the 1960s and then selling to Coca Cola in the 1970s, Peter Newton founded the vineyard with his name at St. Helena in 1977. Then in 2001 LVMH purchased a small share, followed by a majority share (90%) in 2006. Rob Mann came from LVMH's Cape Mentelle property in Margaret River, Australia, to become chief winemaker in 2014 to refresh a winemaking style that had become a little tired.

Newton is a beautiful property with terraced vineyards climbing at all angles on to Spring Mountain above St. Helena. Vineyards occupy less than a quarter of the extensive estate, and extend from 500 to 1,600 feet elevation. The estate is planted with Cabernet Sauvignon (90%) and Merlot. There is also a sizeable vineyard on Mount Veeder, and smaller vineyards in Yountville as well as Carneros and Knights Valley. There is one Cabernet Sauvignon (billed as single vineyard) from each of the three major estates; these represent significantly lower yields than the other cuvées. They are sold only directly from the winery. There is a Bordeaux blend (typically with just over half Cabernet Sauvignon), called Puzzle, from Spring Mountain. Chardonnays come from Knights Valley, Carneros, and Mount Veeder. All the wines are unfiltered, but there is a less expensive range called the Unfiltered, simply labeled as Napa Valley, which includes Cabernet Sauvignon, Pinot Noir, and Chardonnay.

The difference between the ranges is nicely indicated by the Chardonnays: the Napa Unfiltered (a blend from Mount Veeder and Carneros) makes something of a full, rich, traditional impression, but Knights Valley and Carneros are less obvious and have more distinctive characters, the former quite restrained with some herbal impressions, and the latter something of a halfway house with a granular texture. The general house style is on the tight side when young. The Cabernets have tannins that are firm but not aggressive; fruits tend to tautness and elegance but take several years to emerge from their youthful tightness. The Yountville is perhaps the most approachable of the single vineyards.

Nickel & Nickel *

 8164 St. Helena Highway, Oakville, CA 94562
 (1) 707 967 9600
 Darice Spinelli
@ info@nickelandnickel.com
 www.nickelandnickel.com
 Oakville
 Rutherford, Quarry Cabernet Sauvignon
 $80

[map p. 50]

Nickel & Nickel displays its origin as a farm with horses in a paddock alongside route 29, and a series of barns behind, which contain tasting rooms, storage facilities, and the winery. The heart of the property is the Sullenger House, originally built in the 1880s, and now used for reception. Together with the surrounding vineyard, the property was purchased by Gil and Beth Nickel, the owners of Nickel & Nickel (just close by) in 1997. A majority stake in both Nickel & Nickel and Far Niente was sold to GI Partners, a San Francisco private equity firm, in 2016.

Nickel & Nickel focuses on a series of 100% varietal single vineyard wines. Cabernet is the heart, with fifteen different wines representing vineyards in seven of the Napa AVAs. There are also three Merlots from Napa AVAs, a Syrah from Russian River, and three Chardonnays from Carneros and Russian River. Individual vineyards vary from 2-25 acres; sources include estate grapes and long term contracts with growers. "When we say single vineyard, we mean single varietal as well. We do that because we don't want you to see a difference because there's a change in the blend. We want to showcase the vineyard, so we try to reduce the variables, we can't use a lot of the techniques that people use," says winemaker Darice Spinelli.

Defining a house style would be difficult with the range of vineyards; just a sample shows the extent of variety, from stern Hayne vineyard in St. Helena, elegant velvety Quarry vineyard in Rutherford, savory impressions from Copper Streak Vineyard in Stags Leap, and restrained tautness in Sori Bricco from Diamond Mountain. Within Oakville, Rock Cairn Vineyard is finely textured but aromatic, Branding Iron is smoother and softer, and John Sullenger is stern but promises elegance. The single vineyard wines offer an unusual opportunity to compare different parts of Napa, and even different sites in Oakville or Rutherford, with minimal variation aside from source.

Opus One   ***

  7900 St. Helena Highway, Oakville, CA 94562
  (1) 707 944 9442
  Michael Silacci
  info@opusonewinery.com
  www.opusonewinery.com
  Oakville
  Opus One
  Ouverture
  $50
  167 acres; 300,000 bottles
[map p. 50]

Created as a joint venture between Robert Mondavi and Baron Philippe de Rothschild in 1979, Opus One was one of the first collaborations between Bordeaux and Napa winemakers. Before Opus One had its own vineyards, grapes came from Mondavi's holding of To Kalon, so the first vintage in 1979 was really more of a super-cuvée than Opus One as it later developed. The wine was made at Mondavi until Opus One's winery was constructed in 1991. Across route 29 from Mondavi, the Opus One winery is a somewhat bunker-like building nestled into the hillside.

The first estate vineyard was established when Mondavi sold the 14 ha Q block of the To Kalon vineyard to the new venture. Further vineyards directly across route 29 were purchased in 1983 and 1984, and another 19 ha of To Kalon were added in 2004. Over the years the vineyards have been steadily replanted at higher vine density with lower-yielding clones.

After Constellation Brands acquired Mondavi in 2004, Opus One became completely independent. "The dissolution of the partnership (between the owners of Opus One) was a catalyst for change," says Michael Silacci. "This is more of an independent operation now." A second wine, Ouverture, is available only at the winery, produced from declassified lots; it is intended to be less structured than Opus One and more approachable in its youth. It's not vintage-dated, and production is around 10%.

"The assumption from the beginning was that there should be a Bordeaux blend," says Michael Silacci, but there's always a high content of Cabernet Sauvignon (usually over 85%). Initially the blend started with Cabernet Franc and Merlot; Malbec was added in 1994 and Petit Verdot was added in 1997. The wine is easy to under-rate in the early years, when it tends to be somewhat dumb, with a touch of austerity. The wine shows beautifully after 10 years, and after 20 years shows increased elegance. The very first vintage remains vibrant today.

Pahlmeyer Winery **

811 St. Helena Highway, St. Helena, CA 94574
(1) 707 255 2321
Jayson Pahlmeyer
info@pahlmeyer.com
www.pahlmeyer.com
Atlas Peak
Napa Proprietary Red

71 acres; 96,000 bottles
[map p. 50]

Pahlmeyer's history recapitulates the flamboyance of the early years in Napa. It started with Jayson Pahlmeyer's intention to make a "California Mouton" at a site in southern Napa. Against advice from the University at Davis that the site was best suited to growing corn, Jayson planted it with Bordeaux varieties, using plant material smuggled in from Bordeaux. The first release of the Proprietary Red was in 1986. Sources have changed, and today it is a blend from the estate vineyard on Atlas Peak together with grapes sourced from other mountain vineyards, particularly Stagecoach Vineyard on Atlas Peak, and Rancho Chimiles in Wooden Valley; following Mouton, it is more than 80% Cabernet Sauvignon with small amounts of all the other Bordeaux varieties. There is also a Merlot, sourced from the estate and Stagecoach.

The style is forceful: even the Merlot is stern and powerful. "We are trying to make another level of California Merlot, planted in cooler spots on the mountain to give it the structure and acidity it needs," says Cleo Pahlmeyer, who is now taking over from her father. So is the reference point still Bordeaux? "Our benchmark is our own wines, and some from other producers," Cleo says. In addition to the Proprietary Red and Merlot, there is a Napa Chardonnay, and two small barrel selections from the estate, available only to the mailing list.

Jayson also wanted to make Pinot Noir: in fact he tried to purchase two grand cru vineyards in Burgundy, but was not allowed to buy them. Helen Turley, who was one of his early winemakers, suggested that he purchase the Wayfarer Ranch on Sonoma Coast, in what has now become the Fort Ross-Seaview AVA. Vineyards were planted with Pinot and Chardonnay in 1998. Wayfarer now produces a Chardonnay, a Pinot Noir blend from the estate, and four single block Pinots, made at their own facility in Sonoma. The forceful style continues at Wayfarer: the Chardonnay is creamy and exotic; the Pinots are earthy, unctuous, and smoky. Alcohol levels are around 14.5% for the Wayfarer wines, but range from 15-16% for the Napa wines. Everything is full-force here; perhaps the best single word to describe the wines is hedonistic.

Philip Togni Vineyard *

3780 Spring Mountain Rd, St. Helena, CA 94574

(1) 707 963 3731

Lisa Togni

tognivyd@wildblue.net

www.philiptognivineyard.com

St. Helena

Cabernet Sauvignon

Tanbark

$0

9 acres; 24,000 bottles

[map p. 49]

Philip Togni was first involved in planting Cabernet Sauvignon in 1959, and worked in a variety of countries before coming to Cuvaison in Napa. He was involved with several mountain vineyards, including Pride and Chappellet (he made the 1969 Chappellet Cabernet, which is considered one of the great successes of the decade), before he started to clear the land for his own vineyard in 1975, when he planted the first 3 acres of Sauvignon Blanc, followed by 1.5 acres of Cabernet Franc in 1981, all on AxR1. By 1985 everything had been replanted on 110 rootstock.

The estate is at the top of Spring Mountain, close to the border between Napa and Sonoma. It's set well back from the road, and you are given detailed instructions on how to find the unmarked driveway (and to lock the gate behind you). Philip's daughter Lisa is now slowly taking over the winemaking. There are three lines of wines: Togni estate, Tanbark (a second label, introduced pretty much right at the beginning, in 1986), and Ca'Togni (only for sweet wine made from Black Hamburg). "We started off saying we wanted to make a Médoc wine," Philip says, and his Cabernet Sauvignon is typically about 86% Cabernet Sauvignon, with the rest from the other three Bordeaux varieties. Merlot is a little under represented in the wine (6%) compared to plantings (15%) because its yields are lower than the other varieties. The current vintage, together with ten year old wines from a library, is offered to subscribers in the Fall. The wines are intended for the long haul.

Pride Mountain Vineyards

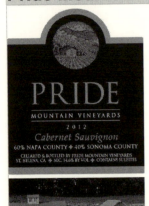

4026 Spring Mountain Road, St. Helena, CA 94574

(1) 707 963 4949

Lacey Olsen

reservations@pridewines.com

www.pridewines.com

Spring Mountain District

Reserve Claret, Cabernet Sauvignon

$30

83 acres; 200,000 bottles

[map p. 49]

Pride is located right at the peak of Spring Mountain. In fact, the vineyards straddle the line between Napa and Sonoma (one inconvenient consequence being that regulations require two bonded wineries, one for handling Napa wines, the other for Sonoma). The origin of every lot has to be tracked. If a wine has more than 75% of grapes from Napa, it can be labeled with the Napa AVA, but most wines carry complicated accounts of the percent coming from Napa County versus Sonoma County.

Vineyards are around 2,000 feet, above the fog line, with 60% on the Sonoma side. Plantings are mostly Bordeaux varieties, with a little Syrah and small amounts of Chardonnay and Viognier. There are three different Cabernet Sauvignons and also a "Claret." The largest production, around 5,000 cases, is the Estate Cabernet Sauvignon, which usually has a bit more fruit from Napa than Sonoma. Winemaker Sally Johnson says this is at its peak for drinking about one year after release, although personally I'd prefer to wait another year.

The two higher tiers are Vintner Select (500-600 cases) and the Reserve Cabernet Sauvignon (1,200 cases). "Vintner Select is the epitome of the California style, flashy and showy, it's 100% Napa," says Sally. It's a 100% Cabernet Sauvignon exclusively from clone 337. The Reserve is a more masculine wine intended for longer aging. "Not many people are making wines like the Reserve," she says. This sometimes has a couple of percent Petit Verdot, and is dominated by Pride's own Rock Arch clone of Cabernet Sauvignon. There's also the Reserve Claret, which is a Merlot-Cabernet Sauvignon blend.

Robert Foley **

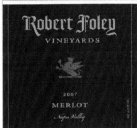

 1300 Summit Lake Drive, Angwin, CA 94508
 (1) 707 965 2669
 Bob Foley
 Bob@RobertFoleyVineyards.com
 www.robertfoleyvineyards.com
 Howell Mountain
 Napa Valley, Cabernet Sauvignon
 $40

[map p. 49]

Bob Foley started working for Heitz in the 1970s, moved to Markham, and then to Pride, and altogether has made 35 vintages in Napa. He started Robert Foley in 1998, with a single wine called Claret. He gained access to more vineyards over the following years, planted his own vineyard, and Claret graduated into a 100% Cabernet because they started bottling the Merlot separately. Until 2003 the wine was a blend, from 2004 to 2005 it had 7% Merlot, since 2006 it has been 100% Cabernet Sauvignon. Production was 500 cases when he started, today it is 8,000 altogether, but it's still a two person company. With 2010 he has gone back to a Bordeaux blend for Claret and will have a separate Cabernet bottling. He is fussy about clones: "Clones of Cabernet are very important. I work with three main clones: the two old clones 4 and 7 are my favorites for masculinity. The newest clone I work with (since 1992) is 337 for its femininity," he says.

Constellation

Robert Mondavi Winery *

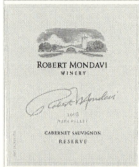

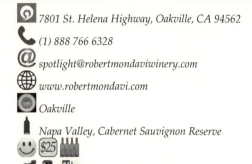

7801 St. Helena Highway, Oakville, CA 94562
(1) 888 766 6328
spotlight@robertmondaviwinery.com
www.robertmondavi.com
Oakville
Napa Valley, Cabernet Sauvignon Reserve
$25
741 acres; 2,700,000 bottles
[map p. 50]

Mondavi scarcely needs any introduction as an icon of Napa Valley. The winery was built in 1966 and the first vintage of Cabernet Sauvignon was released in 1968. The 1974 Reserve Cabernet was one of the wines that put Napa Valley Cabernet on the map. The company broadened out with the introduction in 1979 of the cheaper Woodbridge brand from Lodi. Mondavi continued to be run by the Mondavi family, with Robert's son Tim as winemaker, although it became a publicly quoted company, until it was sold to conglomerate Constellation for $1.36 billion in 2004. (Tim Mondavi now makes wine at his own, company, Continuum: see mini-profile.)

Today Mondavi produces three Cabernet Sauvignons. The Napa Valley bottling is dominated by grapes from To Kalon and Stags Leap District (typically around a third each); Cabernet Sauvignon is 75-85% with Cabernet Franc and Merlot as second in importance. The Oakville bottling is dominated by To Kalon (typically more than three quarters): it has slightly more Cabernet Sauvignon, with Cabernet Franc as the second variety, and small amounts of Merlot, Malbec, and Petit Verdot. The flagship Napa Valley Reserve comes largely (sometimes almost exclusively) from To Kalon. It's usually more than 85% Cabernet Sauvignon; Merlot tended to be the second variety in the early years, but since the mid nineties Cabernet Franc has been second. Petit Verdot made its first appearance in the blend in 1997. In addition, in occasional vintages there is a bottling of a To Kalon Cabernet Sauvignon (from a block of old vines) or a Stags Leap District Cabernet Sauvignon, both 100% varietal. Mondavi also produces Chardonnay, of course, but in some ways is better known for the Fumé Blanc, a Sauvignon Blanc matured in oak barriques; the Reserve To-Kalon bottling has great depth and character, with potential for aging.

Schrader Cellars ★★

4405 Silverado Trail, Calistoga, CA 94515

(1) 707 942 1212

Thomas Brown

info@schradercellars.com

www.schradercellars.com

Calistoga

CCS, Cabernet Sauvignon

0 acres; 22,000 bottles

[map p. 49]

Fred Schrader cofounded Colgin-Schrader Cellars in 1992, and then moved to found Schrader Cellars with his wife Carol in 1998. There are about six cuvées, all Cabernet Sauvignon, coming from grapes purchased from Andy Beckstoffer's top vineyards. The present portfolio concentrates on single vineyard bottlings from To Kalon and the George III vineyard. The wines are among the highest priced from Napa, usually above $350 per bottle on release.

The To Kalon bottlings emphasize small plots within the vineyard, mostly planted with individual clones. The first year of production from To Kalon was 2000, but 2001 was the year when the Schraders moved to an acreage contract, giving them control over issues such as harvesting, which is late, usually at the start of October. The style has always been towards powerful cult wines, ripe, rich, and full, but the massive underlying structure takes them far away from fruit bombs. They use whole berry fermentation, lasting 12-18 days, the wine goes to barrels of new oak just before the end of fermentation (which gives better integration with the wood), then goes through MLF and spends 14-18 months in the wood, which are barrels from Duamaji made for Merlot on the Right Bank of Bordeaux.

The characters of the individual bottlings demonstrate the relative differences between Cabernet Sauvignon clones at a high level of concentration and ripeness, with clone 6 the most structured, 337 the most opulent, and clone 4 the most loose knit. "Clone 337 doesn't have the steely backbone that 4 and 6 have; the wine is more right-bankish and ready to go," Fred says.

It was a surprise when Schrader sold the brand to giant producer Constellation in 2017 (for $60 million). As there are no vineyards, the purchase basically involves the small inventory and the contracts for purchasing grapes. It is uncertain whether and how the brand may change now.

Screaming Eagle Winery ★★★

Silverado Trail, Oakville, CA 94558
(1) 707 944 0749
Armand de Maigret
winery@screamingeagle.com
www.screamingeagle.com
Oakville
Screaming Eagle
② Second Flight
🚫 @
🍇🍇 44 acres; 13,000 bottles
[map p. 50]

Screaming Eagle scarcely needs any introduction: it is by far California's most famous cult wine. The winery was created when Jean Phillips bought 23 ha of land just off the Silverado trail, in the Oakville area, for an unusually high price in 1986. The area was known to the neighbors as providing high quality grapes; largely Riesling, it was replanted to Cabernet Sauvignon in 1987 with small amounts of Merlot and Cabernet Franc. Heidi Barrett was engaged as winemaker. Since then, further replanting, managed by David Abreu, has brought the vineyard into a Bordeaux-like balance of Cabernet Sauvignon, Cabernet Franc, and Merlot.

The slight depression in the land creates a small frost problem from time to time, which is handled by overhead sprinklers fed by a lake. Drainage has been installed under the new plantings to recapture water. They expect to dry farm more or less around two thirds of the ranch, especially where there's more clay (to the west). This is an early ripening site, but even so, they are early pickers here, usually a week to ten days ahead of everyone else. The Cabernet has historically been clones 7 and See, but in the last couple of years some clones 6, 169, and 337 have crept in.

The winery was sold in 2006 to two partners, one of whom has since left. Stanley Kroenke, who made his fortune in agriculture, is now the sole owner. Armand de Maigret manages Screaming Eagle and Kroenke's other wine properties, which include Jonata and The Hilt, in Californian coastal regions, and most recently, Bonneau du Martray in Corton Charlemagne.

Shafer Vineyards

**

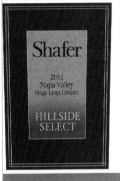

6154 Silverado Trail, Napa, CA 94558

(1) 707 944 2877

John Gretz

info@shafervineyards.com

www.shafervineyards.com

Stags Leap District

Stag's Leap District, Cabernet Sauvignon

$75

205 acres; 384,000 bottles

[map p. 50]

John Shafer left a career in corporate publishing to move to Napa Valley, where he purchased 210 acres and planted vineyards in 1972 in what became the Stags Leap District in 1989. The first vintage in 1978 used Cabernet Sauvignon from the Sunspot vineyard that rises up immediately above the winery. Hillside Select started in 1983, when Doug Shafer became winemaker. "I was tasting lots and the Sunspot was head and shoulders above everything else. I thought we should bottle it separately—this became the 1982 Reserve. That started the program. I got tired of explaining what Reserve was, because everyone had a reserve, and in 1983 we called it Hillside Select. The fruits are so good you can keep your hands off it—Hillside Select is the easiest wine to make," Doug says.

There are about 20 ha on the hillside block, and the best lots are selected each year for Hillside Select, of which there are usually 2,000-2,500 cases. It's 100% Cabernet Sauvignon. There are also about 8,000 cases of the One Point Five Cabernet Sauvignon, which comes from the hillside estate vineyard and the Borderline vineyard two miles south of Shafer at the edge of the Stags Leap District. Other wines include Chardonnay, Merlot, and Syrah. The style is rich and lush, distinctly New World, for all the wines, although Hillside Select seems to have toned down a little with recent vintages.

Robert Sinskey Vineyards *

6320 Silverado Trail, Napa, CA 94558

(1) 707 944 9090

Conner Burns or Phil Abram

rsv@robertsinskey.com

www.robertsinskey.com

Stags Leap District

Carneros, Four Vineyards, Pinot Noir

$40

200 acres; 275,000 bottles

[map p. 50]

The modern winery is located on the Silverado Trail in Napa Valley, but the vineyards are in Carneros, where Sinskey has four Pinot Noir vineyards (there is also a vineyard in Sonoma). About half of all production is Pinot Noir, making Sinskey a Pinot Noir specialist in the area. Wines are made only from estate fruit. At one point the vineyards were all heirloom selections, but after phylloxera they were replanted with Dijon and Pommard. Rob is now looking for more heirloom selections. "Dijon clones produce ripe fruit and lower acid, usually showy, but missing what I go to Pinot Noir for."

Until 2001 Sinskey made a Carneros Pinot Noir and a reserve bottling, but felt that "Reserve" had little meaning since the wines were not produced in a rich oaky style, so the change was made to single vineyard bottlings. Rob sees the winery as a bridge between old and new worlds. "Russian River is the competition in the markets, but stylistically the competition is Burgundy or Oregon." The vineyards have different characters, and harvest dates for Pinot are spread over about four weeks. There is complete destemming for all wines, cap irrigation during fermentation rather than punch-down to give better control of extraction, and maturation in 30% new oak. The wines are intended to drink well from soon after the vintage, and Rob says that he sees about ten years as the natural life span for most vintages.

Carneros is the entry-level Pinot, made in a more forward style than is intended to drink sooner. Four Vineyards is a blend from each of Sinskey's individual Pinot Noir vineyards: it's more elegant than the Carneros blend, but has less personality than the single vineyard wines. Vandal vineyard, on the hillside of Northern Carneros close to the town of Napa, is the first to pick and the leanest. "Its characteristic note is the bright fruit with a cranberry essence," Rob says. The Three Amigos vineyard is right off the San Pablo Bay, just by the Napa marina; usually the last to be harvested, it's more rounded and less acid. Capa is a small vineyard in the sunniest location; planted mostly with Dijon clones, it is usually the most "Californian" in style of Sinskey's Pinot Noirs, with more black than red fruits.

Spottswoode Estate Vineyard & Winery *

 1902 Madrona Avenue, St. Helena, CA 94574

 (1) 707 963 0134

 Beth Novak Milliken

 estate@spottswoode.com

 www.spottswoode.com

 St. Helena

 St. Helena, Cabernet Sauvignon

 Lyndenhurst

 $75

39 acres; 84,000 bottles

[map p. 50]

Driving along Madrona Avenue in downtown St. Helena through suburban housing, you wonder where the Spottswoode winery can be, and then suddenly you come out into 15 hectares of vineyards that stretch from the edge of the town up to the mountains. Jack and Mary Novak purchased the property in 1972, and were refused a permit to make wine because the neighborhood was residential. The later purchase (in 1990) of a winery across the road allowed the wine to be made in the vicinity.

The Cabernet Sauvignon is a blend, although there is no Merlot. "We don't have any Merlot growing here, I'm not a fan of Merlot in this area. There was some Merlot at Spottswoode long ago, but it was removed," says winemaker Aron Weinkauf. In addition to 12.5 ha of Cabernet Sauvignon, there are 1.25 ha of Cabernet Franc and 0.4 ha of Petit Verdot for the blend, and also a hectare of Sauvignon Blanc. A second wine, called Lyndenhurst, is made in a more approachable fruit-forward, less ageworthy style (using 60% new oak compared to Spottswoode's 68%). Production is usually about 3,000 cases of Spottswoode and 700 cases of Lyndenhurst. My favorite vintage of Spottswoode is the 1992.

Stag's Leap Wine Cellars *

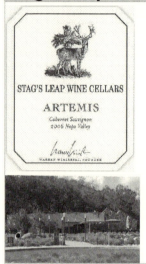

5766 Silverado Trail, Napa CA 94558

(1) 707 944 2020

Marcus Notaro

retail@cask23.com

www.cask23.com

Stags Leap District

Fay Vineyard, Cabernet Sauvignon

$45

239 acres; 1,800,000 bottles
[map p. 49]

Stag's Leap Wine Cellars has a special place in the history of Napa for gaining first place for its 1973 Cabernet in the Judgment of Paris tasting in Paris in 1976. Coming ahead of three first growth Bordeaux from the 1970 vintage, this stamped Napa Valley Cabernet as a serious contender on the world stage. Stag's Leap had been started by Warren Winiarski only just previously, when he purchased a 44 acre plot that he planted as a vineyard in 1970, now known as the SLV (Stag's Leap Vineyard). So 1973 was his first vintage.

Subsequently two wines from Stag's Leap became established as leaders: Cask 23 and Fay's Vineyard. In fact, the original plot had been purchased on the basis of Warren's tasting of wines that had been made from the adjacent Fay vineyard, which Stag's Leap later purchased (in 1986). Cask 23 is based on a election of the best lots from SLV (60%) and Fay's Vineyard (40%); and single vineyard wines are made from both SLV and Fay's. Fay's vineyard tends to have a softer, more perfumed elegance, while SLV is a bigger wine, with more exotic fruit notes.

In 1996 the vineyard holdings were much expanded by purchasing the 128 acre Arcadia vineyard farther north in Napa Valley. Today a new visitor center has been built in the vineyards. In addition to the top level wines, there's also a mid-level range under the name of Napa Valley Collection and a line or cheaper wines under the Hawk Crest label. In 2007, the winery was sold to a partnership of Chateau Ste. Michelle and Antinori, and since then has somewhat lost its luster. Recent vintages of SLV have been awfully soft for a wine with such a distinguished history. "Too oaky, too fruity, too soft: the very model of a modern Napa Cabernet," my tasting notes say for the most recent vintage. Perhaps the recent arrival of Marcus Notaro from Col Solare (another Ste. Michelle property) will change things.

Staglin Family Vineyard　　　　　　　　　　　　　　　　　　　　　　　*

1570 Bella Oaks Ln, Rutherford, CA 94573
(1) 707 944 0477
Lindsay Dale
info@staglinfamily.com
www.staglinfamily.com
Rutherford
Rutherford Cabernet Sauvignon
Napa, Salus Chardonnay
Salus
$75
44 acres; 96,000 bottles [map p. 50]

Staglin is one of the wave of wineries founded in the 1980s by people who had been successful elsewhere and decided they wanted to make wine. The old estate had gone through many owners, turned to producing prunes during Prohibition, and then later became part of Beaulieu (contributing to the Georges de Latour Private Reserve), until the Staglins purchased it in 1985. It is right under the Mayacamas Mountains; indeed, the winery, finished in 2002, is a series of tunnels hollowed out into the mountain. The visitor center is in a historic house that was on the property and has been restored.

The estate is 60 acres, but also makes wine from other sources. After the Bella Oaks Vineyard (formerly the basis for a Cabernet Sauvignon from Heitz) was sold to the Booth family in 2010, the Staglins started to produce the Booth Bella Oaks cuvée. In 2015 they shared a purchase of the adjacent Fahrig Ranch, which is planted with Cabernet Sauvignon. David Abreu manages the vineyards; Michel Rolland consults on winemaking. The focus is Cabernet Sauvignon and Chardonnay, with top wines labeled simply as Staglin Family Estate. Salus is a second label, introduced in 1995, but the Staglins do not regard it as a second wine. "The difference is stylistic: based on selection of barrels that are softer and more straightforward, Salus is intended to be more approachable. Staglin is more complex and structural."

Salus is a smaller production than Staglin. The Cabernet Sauvignons usually include very small amounts of other Bordeaux varieties, but the general impression for both labels is full-force varietal. The wine ages relatively quickly, beginning to show tertiary notes after about five years: the Staglins see the sweet spot for the estate Cabernet as ten years after release. The Chardonnay has been similarly intense, with phenolics on the finish, but "We are moving away from what people think of as the California style—buttery and rich—towards more of a fresh fruit style for the Chardonnay." It includes grapes from the Hudson and Hyde vineyards in Carneros. The general house style is rich and oxidative, although for both Chardonnay and Cabernet, Staglin is more muted compared to Salus by a sense of structure in the background.

Trefethen Vineyards *

1160 Oak Knoll Avenue, Napa, CA 94558
(1) 707 255 7700
Janet Trefethen
winery@trefethen.com
www.trefethen.com
Oak Knoll
Oak Knoll Cabernet Sauvignon
Oak Knoll Chardonnay
$25
439 acres; 720,000 bottles
[map p. 49]

When Gene and Katie Trefethen purchased the estate in 1968 it was essentially in mothballs. When grapevines died they had been replaced by fruit trees. So everything had to be restored. Gene had just retired from builder Kaiser Industries, and his intention was to grow grapes. That's still reflected in about a quarter of the grapes being sold off. However, the next generation, John and Janet Trefethen, prompted the move into winemaking, with the first vintage in 1973. The third generation, Loren and Hailey, is now involved. The main estate is on the flat, just off route 29; there is a smaller estate in the foothills of the Mayacamas. The original winery was built in 1866; it was damaged in the earthquake of 2014 and is being restored to provide a storage facility. Wine is made in the new winery, built in the 1980s.

When the Trefethens bought the estate they asked UC Davis what to plant: UC Davis asked, "how much land do you have," and when they heard the answer said " Well, just plant everything and see what works." That is still reflected in an unusually wide range of wines, with twenty cuvées including Merlots, Cabernets, Malbec, Chardonnays, and Rieslings. "There are not many places in Napa where you can have the diversity of grapes we grow here in Oak Knoll," says winemaker Brian Kays. "We farm the whites for freshness, for reds it is almost the opposite because we are in a cool spot." Asked what is the most typical wine here, Brian says, "It would be between the Merlot and the Cabernet but probably the Cabernet; this has a number of things important to Trefethen, it gives the preponderance of fruit but also herbal and spice impressions. And you can taste Oak Knoll in all these wines, by which I mean that you can see the freshness and brightness of acidity."

Few of the wines are monovarietals: the Cabernet usually contains about 10% of Malbec and Petit Verdot, the Merlot usually has some Malbec and Cabernet. Use of oak is idiosyncratic, based on French but often including some American and Hungarian; new oak is about 40% for the Merlot and 50% for the Cabernet. Dragon's Tooth is a proprietary red based on Malbec with a lot of Petit Verdot, and is the most aromatic of the red cuvées. The Malbec is a monovarietal expressing the sleek character of the variety. Among whites, the Estate Chardonnay is the most representative as it is a blend from across the whole estate, while Harmony comes from a specific plot and offers a less obvious but richer impression. Both show cool climate character, however. There are two Rieslings—"We are the largest producer of Riesling in Napa," Brian says—a dry Riesling (which actually contains a touch of residual sugar) and a late harvest (made by committing a small plot of the vineyard to wait for botrytis). It's hard to define a house style across such a wide range, but it's fair to say it achieves the aim of representing the (relatively) fresher character of Oak Knoll.

Turnbull Wine Cellars *

8210 St. Helena Highway, CA 94562
(1) 800 887 6285
Peter Heitz
reservations@turnbullwines.com
www.turnbullwines.com
Oakville
Oakville, Fortuna Cabernet Sauvignon

165 acres; 192,000 bottles
[map p. 50]

William Turnbull was an architect in San Francisco who bought the first vineyard in the 1970s, when there was just a farmhouse on the property. In 1993 Patrick O'Dell bought the property; his daughter Zoe Johns is now the owner and general manager. The original winery right on route 29 has now become the tasting room, and the present winery (a somewhat practical building) runs back from it. Turnbull has four vineyards: the small home estate surrounds the winery, to the east beyond the Silverado Trail there are the Fortuna Vineyard and Leopoldina (at 1,000 foot elevation). There is also a vineyard in Calistoga.

The focus is on red wine, mostly Cabernet Sauvignon; the only white is Sauvignon Blanc. Only two wines are in general distribution: a Sauvignon Blanc and the Napa Valley Cabernet. The premium wines, coming from individual vineyards, are available only from the winery or through the wine club. There are individual Cabernets from each vineyard and three separate cuvées from plots within Leopoldina. The flagship wine is the Black Label Cabernet, which is a barrel selection of the most powerful lots from all the vineyards, "structured around the heart of darkness," says winemaker Peter Heitz. Nominally the Cabernets are blends, but Cabernet Sauvignon is rarely less than 96%. "In big vintages I might add some Cabernet Franc or Merlot, in vintages needing more oomph I would use Petit Verdot or Malbec," Peter says. New oak is around 50% for the single vineyard wines. "The vineyards have a big influence, style is more a matter of source than due to the house."

The wines tend to be faintly aromatic, in the direction of violets, forceful but not overwhelming, certainly taut, giving a tight impression when young. Fortuna is the most feminine and shows best when young; Leopoldina is more backward and brooding. Black Label has a sheen of refinement over and above the single vineyard wines. Peter does not take a position on whether the wines should be drinkable immediately or it should be necessary to wait, but for my palate the power of Oakville is evident and most wines need three or four years after release.

Viader Vineyards

1120 Deer Park Road, Deer Park, CA 94576
(1) 707 963 3816
Delia Viader
tastings@viader.com
www.viader.com
Howell Mountain
Proprietary Red
$75
29 acres; 60,000 bottles
[map p. 49]

Viader Vineyards occupies a steep slope on Howell Mountain that runs down into Bell Canyon. It's at an elevation of 1,200 feet, just below the Howell Mountain AVA. Purchased and then cleared in 1981, the land was planted with Cabernet Sauvignon, Cabernet Franc, and Petit Verdot. There's no Merlot or Malbec because they do not do well in the mountain environment. "I planted Petit Verdot thinking it would go into the Proprietary Red but it just didn't fit," says Delia Viader, explaining why Viader's blend is solely Cabernet Sauvignon and Cabernet Franc. "Differences between the wines are more vintage driven than by variety per se because I change the blend with the vintage," she says.

Cabernet Sauvignon is always a majority, varying from 51-75% over the past decade. The Petit Verdot goes into a monovarietal wine, as does any Cabernet Franc that isn't used for the Proprietary Red; there's also a blended wine that is largely Cabernet Sauvignon and Syrah. Other wines are made from purchased fruit. A change in style may occur as Alex Viader takes over, as he prefers more intensity and extraction. The 2012 shows more power and intensity than previously, but retains that characteristic chocolaty smoothness coming from the Cabernet Franc, and making Viader a distinctive wine.

Vineyard 29 *

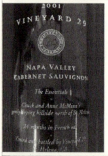

 2929 Highway 29 North, St. Helena, CA 94574

📞 (1) 707 963 9292

Austin Gallion

@ austin@vineyard29.com

🌐 www.vineyard29.com

St. Helena

Napa, 29 Estate Cabernet Sauvignon

$135

29 acres; 100,000 bottles

[map p. 50]

The question driving Vineyard 29 since Chuck and Anne McMinn purchased the property in 2000 has been, "What's the maximum amount of wine I can make and stay at 95 points?" Wine production started at the small vineyard surrounding the winery when the previous owners were persuaded by their neighbors to plant some vines. Success overwhelmed them, and full commercial operation started only with the change of ownership.

The striking post-modern winery was built in 2003 on the elevated site just north of St. Helena with views across to the Vaca Mountains on the other side of the valley. The cave goes back into the mountain behind. There is a tasting room in downtown Napa. The original 2.5 acres at the winery were expanded to 24 acres, and Aida vineyard two miles to the north, previously planted to Zinfandel, was added and mostly replanted to Cabernet.

The winery's capacity of 12,000 cases is split between two ranges. Vineyard 29 wines are exclusively estate production, with six different wines, ranging from 50-700 cases per year. The Cru range comes from purchased grapes, including Napa Cabernet Sauvignon sourced from a variety of vineyards, Sauvignon Blanc, and Willamette Pinot Noir. Vineyard 29 wines are sold almost entirely directly by the winery, but Cru is in general distribution (the Cabernet goes mostly to restaurants).

The home estate produces three varietal wines: Cabernet Sauvignon, Cabernet Franc, and Sauvignon Blanc. The Aida vineyard produces Cabernet Sauvignon, Zinfandel (from 45 year-old vines), and a Late Harvest Zinfandel. House style is refined and elegant with a very fine texture, showing quite sweet impressions with lifted aromatics at the end, so the tannins fade into the background. The house style carries through the varieties, with Zinfandel showing more aromatics but not overwhelming (perhaps aided by 15% of Cabernet Sauvignon and Petit Syrah), Cabernet Sauvignon tending to blackcurrants, and Cabernet Franc showing more muted fruits. Austin Gallion at Vineyard 29 says that, "Usually Aida is more muscular and the Estate 29 wines are more refined, but it can vary with the vintage." The 2013 vintage proved so powerful that it was released after the 2014.

ZD Wines

8383 Silverado Trail, Napa, CA 94558
(1) 707 963 5188
Chris Musante or Barbie Jamieson
info@zdwines.com
www.zdwines.com
Rutherford
Carneros Pinot Noir
$40
37 acres; 360,000 bottles
[map p. 50]

Brett DeLeuze's father came from aerospace to start the winery with partner Gino Zepponi in 1969, but became sole owner when Gino died in 1985. Members of the DeLeuze family are involved at all levels from winemaking to marketing. The estate started with a 34 acre property in Carneros, where wine was made at weekends; the small property on the Silverado Trail in Rutherford was purchased in 1978; and the winery was built in 1993.

ZD makes wine from three varieties: Pinot Noir, Chardonnay, and Cabernet Sauvignon. "With each we make what we consider to be our traditional white label and a reserve wine," Brett says. Typically the white label is based on purchased grapes, and the Reserve comes from the estate.

The white label Chardonnay comes from very varied sources. "We've gone in the opposite direction from most people in making a blend of Chardonnay from four regions, Napa, Carneros-Sonoma, Monterey, and Santa Maria Valley," Brett explains. "We believe the blend is more complex than any one region would be." It showcases rich, tropical fruits, emphasized by fermentation at very low temperature. The Chardonnay Reserve comes from the estate in Carneros and is less forceful. The Pinot Noirs come from Carneros, showing aromatics of earthy strawberries, but Founders Reserve is less overt.

There are three Cabernet Sauvignons: the white label Napa includes a little Petit Verdot; the Founders Reserve is exclusively Cabernet, and Abacus is unusually based on a solera system. The rationale is that the DeLeuze's feel that the increasing complexity of old Cabernet is accompanied by too much loss of fruit. So Abacus is a blend that includes Cabernet Sauvignon from every vintage, kept in old oak barrels. Every year the latest three vintages are added to it to increase volume by 20% and then 15% is drawn off for the current bottling: 2015 is the 18th release. The white label Cabernet is straightforward, the Reserve shows more structure. and Abacus shows much increased refinement. The general house style is sweet and ripe with strong aromatics, reinforced by extensive use of American oak. "We want flavorful delicious wines," is how Brett describes the style.

Sonoma

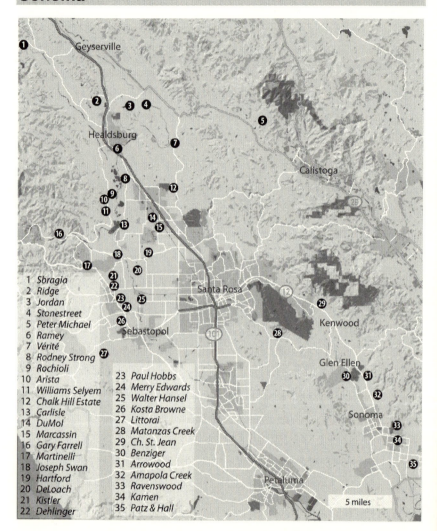

1 Sbragia
2 Ridge
3 Jordan
4 Stonestreet
5 Peter Michael
6 Ramey
7 Vérité
8 Rodney Strong
9 Rochioli
10 Arista
11 Williams Selyem
12 Chalk Hill Estate
13 Carlisle
14 DuMol
15 Marcassin
16 Gary Farrell
17 Martinelli
18 Joseph Swan
19 Hartford
20 DeLoach
21 Kistler
22 Dehlinger
23 Paul Hobbs
24 Merry Edwards
25 Walter Hansel
26 Kosta Browne
27 Littorai
28 Matanzas Creek
29 Ch. St. Jean
30 Benziger
31 Arrowood
32 Amapola Creek
33 Ravenswood
34 Kamen
35 Patz & Hall

Amapola Creek ★★

392 London Way, Sonoma, CA 95476
(1) 707 938 3783
David DuBois
reservations@aristawinery.com
amapolacreek.com
Sonoma Valley
Cabernet Sauvignon

19 acres; 36,000 bottles
[map p. 112]

I was extremely careful not to arrive too early when I visited Richard Arrowood at his new winery, Amapola Creek, just below the Monte Rosso vineyard. During a visit to Monte Rosso earlier, the crew had mentioned that Richard was a well known gun collector, and I was anxious not to be treated as a trespasser. I arrived to be greeted by Richard with his arm in a sling; he had an accident when requalifying for his concealed gun permit.

Richard Arrowood is a legendary winemaker. He started at Chateau St. Jean, where he stayed from 1974 to 1990, when he left to run his own winery, the eponymous Arrowood, which he had started in 1986. After Arrowood was sold to Mondavi, and then changed hands multiple times following Constellation's purchase of Mondavi, Richard moved on to another winery, Amapola Creek. He had bought the site and planted a vineyard in 2000, with the intention of selling grapes, but decided when he left Arrowood to make the wine himself.

With the same red volcanic soils as the Monte Rosso Vineyard, Amapola Creek is a 40 ha ranch on the western slopes of the mountain; the vineyards are planted with French clones of Cabernet Sauvignon and a little Petit Verdot, Syrah, and Grenache. Around 85-90% of production is red. The first Cabernet Sauvignon vintage in 2005 was 100% varietal; in 2006 and 2007, a little Petit Verdot was included. The Cabernet is a blend of four different vineyard plots. The most promising vintage in my tasting was the 2006.

Kendall - Jackson

Arrowood Winery ★★

📍 14347 Sonoma Highway, Glen Ellen, CA 95442
📞 (1) 707 935 2600
Kristina Shideler
@ hospitality@arrowoodvineyards.com
🌐 www.arrowoodvineyards.com
Sonoma Valley
Reserve Speciale, Cabernet Sauvignon
$15 @
19 acres; 250,000 bottles
[map p. 112]

Richard Arrowood bought land in 1986 and built his winery in 1987, focusing on varietal wines coming from various sites in Sonoma, sourced from a variety of growers; the vineyards surrounding the winery were known as Richard's spice box, and consist of just 3.6 ha of Bordeaux varieties that are used for blending with Cabernet Sauvignon. In 2000, Richard Arrowood sold the winery to Mondavi, but stayed on as winemaker. After Constellation Brands purchased Mondavi, they sold off Arrowood at the end of 2004.

A troubled period followed as the winery changed hands until it ended up as part of Jackson Family Vineyards in 2010. The original facility remains in Sonoma Valley, but wine production has been shifted to Jackson's central facility at Cardinale in Oakville in Napa Valley. Richard Arrowood moved on to found a new winery, and Heidi von der Mehden took over winemaking. The top wines here, which share the same price point, are the Monte Rosso single vineyard designate and the Réserve Spéciale, a blend made most years from sources that change depending on the vintage. The Reserve was a blend until 1994, and then became a hundred percent Cabernet Sauvignon.

Carlisle Winery & Vineyards *

6301 Starr Rd, Windsor, CA 95492

(1) 707 836 7500

Mike Officer

wine@carlislewinery.com

www.carlislewinery.com

Russian River Valley

Sonoma Valley, Pagani Ranch Zinfandel

$15

19 acres; 120,000 bottles [map p. 112]

"I'm a bit of a grape junky, I'm fascinated by fruit and vineyards and the resulting wines," says Mike Officer, explaining why he produces around 25 cuvées, with an average lot size only around 400 cases. Starting on a small basis by making wine at his home, he slowly increased production through the first commercial vintage in 1998, and finally gave up his day job to make wine full time in 2004. Wine was made in a custom press facility until he was able to purchase the winery, a rather barebones warehouse facility, in 2012. Although he owns Carlisle vineyard, and leases some others, most grapes are purchased from other sources, from as far south as Paso Robles to as far north as Mendocino, but "We are mostly a Russian River producer."

Passionate about old vines, Mike helped to found a society for preserving historical vineyards; and many of his cuvées come from very old vineyards, often a century old. About half of production is old vines Zinfandel, or to be more accurate, field blends with Zinfandel as the predominant variety. "It's by far the hardest of all the varieties I've ever worked with, it's very difficult to make into great wine," Mike says, "We have to be true to the variety and let Zin be Zin, but not to get out of hand and become too wild and rambunctious. Our wines are all obvious Zinfandels but they have structure and acidity."

Winemaking is consistent. "We make Zinfandel like Pinot Noir but it is all de-stemmed, we maximize whole berries, cold soak for 5-6 days in small open top fermenters, pump-over at first, followed by punch down at the end. The wine goes into barrel, we wait until the Spring for MLF, and then rack and bottle. New oak is about 17%." Zinfandels vary from the lively aromatics of Pagani Ranch in Sonoma Valley, to the taut impression of the active acidity of Russian River's Mancini Ranch, to the restrained aromatics of Dry Creek Valley, and the almost stern character of Dupratt from high on Mendocino Ridge.

Mike is also interested in Rhône varieties—"I'm a huge fan of Grange des Pères, but it's become very expensive so I thought, why not make my own?"—and his homage to the Languedoc comes with Two Acres (a field blend based on Mourvèdre that he discovered in an old vineyard in Russian River) and The Integral (Mourvèdre and Syrah cofermented from n vineyard high in Bennett Valley). Two Acres has a traditional structure and restraint, while The Integral shows a more modern style of overt fruits. The house style shows the intensity of old vines, with variations reflecting the source and field blend.

Chalk Hill Estate *

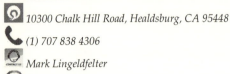 10300 Chalk Hill Road, Healdsburg, CA 95448

📞 (1) 707 838 4306

 Mark Lingeldfelter

@ concierge@chalkhill.com

🌐 www.chalkhill.com

Sonoma Valley

Russian River, Cabernet-Malbec

Sonoma County, Chardonnay

375 acres; 420,000 bottles

[map p. 112]

The Chalk Hill Estate shows in microcosm the diversity of terroirs in this sub-AVA within Russian River Valley, going from warm, south-facing areas resembling Bordeaux to cool north-facing areas that resemble Alsace. "Bordeaux varieties only really ripen here in just the right sites, it's much cooler than Napa," says vineyard manager Mark Lingenfelder. Chalk Hill Estate was 50% Pinot Noir in the mid eighties, but the sites that are suitable for black grapes are really too warm for Pinot. The estate today is a mix of white varieties (mostly Chardonnay with a little Sauvignon Blanc) and Bordeaux varieties.

The Cabernet is planted on the tops of warm south-facing slopes where the soil is based on red volcanic rocks. There is an unusually high concentration of the old varieties, mostly Malbec (9 ha), with a little Carmenère (1 ha). This has led to the production of some unusual blends, Cabernet/Malbec, Cabernet/Carmenère, Merlot/Malbec, and a Cabernet/Petit Verdot named for the new proprietor, W. P Foley, who purchased Chalk Hill in 2010. The estate wine used to be labeled as Cabernet Sauvignon, but lost the varietal label when the proportion of Cabernet fell below 75% as the result of planting more Malbec. Judging from the massive character and very high alcohol levels of the wines, you would never guess that this was a relatively cool climate for Cabernet. It wasn't really clear to me whether the difference between the relatively open Cabernet/Carmenère and the somewhat closed Cabernet/Malbec was due to the minor variety (20% Carmenère or 10% Malbec) or the source of the Cabernet Sauvignon, as I had not expected the Malbec to bring so much more structure than the Carmenère.

Treasury Wine Estates

Chateau St. Jean

8555 Sonoma Highway, Kenwood, CA 95452

(1) 707 833 4134

Michael McNeil

cs_chateaustjean@chateaustjean.com

www.chateaustjean.com

Sonoma Valley

Cinq Cepages

$15

91 acres; 3,000,000 bottles

[map p. 112]

Founded in 1973, Chateau St. Jean was a pioneer for producing single vineyard designate wines. "The owners of Chateau St. Jean asked me to do vineyard designates like the Burgundians do," says Richard Arrowood, Chateau St. Jean's legendary first winemaker (who left in 1990). Chateau St. Jean was best known for its single vineyard Chardonnays, at one time as many as nine, although red wine was a major focus, with emphasis on Cabernet Sauvignon, until 1980. There was a pause in red wine production in the early eighties, and then it resumed with a blended wine based on Cabernet Sauvignon. When phylloxera forced replanting, the estate was about 80 ha, with about half planted, mostly with white varieties, but replanting focused on black varieties. "We were set on producing a blended wine, using all five Bordeaux varieties, which was close to impossible at the time," says current winemaker Margo Van Staaveren, who has been at Chateau St. Jean for thirty years, and saw the ownership change when it was sold to Beringer in 1996. Production has been moved to Beringer's headquarters in Napa.

1990 was the first vintage of Cinq Cepages. "Cabernet Sauvignon has varied from 75-83%; the next most frequent variety is usually Merlot today, although previously it was Cabernet Franc. Malbec and Petit Verdot are used in small amounts because they have such varietal expression that otherwise they would dominate the blend," she says. About half of the grapes comes from vineyards owned by Chateau St. Jean, but outside the home estate, so sources may include Sonoma Valley, Alexander Valley, Knights Valley, Dry Creek Valley, and Russian River Valley, depending on the year. Until 2007, the wine carried a varietal label as Cabernet Sauvignon, but that was removed as of 2008. "This had been the intent from the beginning. We put Cabernet Sauvignon on the label at the beginning because we were so closely identified with white wine," Margo says.

Dehlinger Winery *

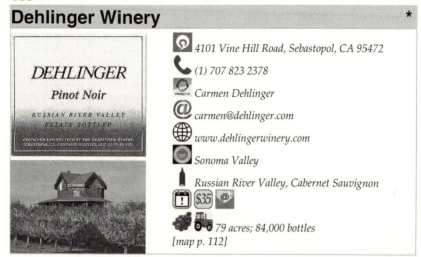

4101 Vine Hill Road, Sebastopol, CA 95472
(1) 707 823 2378
Carmen Dehlinger
carmen@dehlinger.com
www.dehlingerwinery.com
Sonoma Valley
Russian River Valley, Cabernet Sauvignon
$35
79 acres; 84,000 bottles
[map p. 112]

Tom Dehlinger studied winemaking and viticulture at Davis in 1970; he thought he would make wine as a hobby, but it took over. The vineyard was a pioneering effort. "I bought this parcel in 1973 and planted the first 14 acres in 1975 with the best varieties of the time, Pinot Noir, Chardonnay, Gewürztraminer, Riesling. The Riesling was regrafted to Chardonnay a year later. Two acres of Cabernet were planted using a virus free clone in 1975, on AxR1 like all the others," he recollects. "We started our second planting with 3.5 acres of Cabernet Franc, we planted 5 more acres of Cabernet Sauvignon, and in 1988 we planted 3 acres of Merlot. The experiment was partly successful and partly unsuccessful."

At first the Cabernet Sauvignon was vinified as a monovarietal wine, there were Cabernet Sauvignon-Merlot blends between 1992 and 1997 (the Cabernet Franc was too herbal to be included), and since 1998 the Cabernet Sauvignon has been a monovarietal. Today there are two bottlings of Cabernet Sauvignon; varietal-labeled from the best areas, and since 2002 a Claret from the lesser areas. My favorite was the Bordeaux blend from 1995.

Today Pinot Noir makes up half of plantings, and is what the winery is best known for. Chardonnay is in second place, and Cabernet Sauvignon only in third. Pinot was planted in two waves, from 1975-1989 and then again from 2011-2014. They are mostly the Pommard and Swan clones. Usually there are about 25 lots of Pinot Noir, and they are blended into two cuvées, named for the major soil types: Goldridge (more red fruits) and Altamont (more black fruits and some whole bunch clusters used during fermentation). There are several special cuvées from old vines or specific plots.

The estate expanded in 2017 by buying another 35 acres of an adjacent property. Most of the grapes are presently sold off, so wine is made from about 50 acres altogether. Tom's daughter Eva is slowly taking over winemaking, and another daughter, Carmen, is taking over sales and marketing from her mother, Carole.

Gary Farrell Wines *

🜨 10701 Westside Road, Healdsburg CA 95448
📞 (1) 707 473 2900
@ debbie_farrell@adsw.com
🌐 www.garyfarrellwines.com
Russian River Valley
Russian River Valley, Starr Ridge, Pinot Noir
☺ $35 🏭
🚜

[map p. 112]

Gary Farrell became involved in winemaking in the Russian River Valley in the 1970s and began to make his own wine in 1982. The model was based on purchasing fruit from top vineyard sites, including Rochioli and the adjacent Allen vineyard. A winery was built in 2000 in a beautiful location overlooking Westside Road with a spectacular view of the area. The winery had a troubled period after it passed through several owners following a sale in 2004. In 2011 it ended up with investor group Vincraft, which also owned Kosta Browne. Gary Farrell left in 2009 to start another winery.

Currently the winery produces 4,000 cases of Russian River Valley selection, 1,000 cases from Carneros fruit from sister company Buena Vista, and 2,400 cases of single vineyard Pinot Noirs. Typically Pinot Noir is about 60% of production and Chardonnay about 30%. Winemaker Susan Reed says that they want the wines to be fruit driven so they pick a little earlier than most in order to get lower alcohol. "We want people to be able to tell the wines are Gary Farrell." There is complete destemming, 5-7 days cold soak, and fermentation until pressing off at 1 degree Brix; all the press wine usually goes into the Russian River Valley bottling. This gets 30% new oak, and the single vineyard wines get 40%. Of the Russian River wines, Hallberg is a bigger, darker wine, with black, richer fruits (partly reflecting the Dijon clones), whereas Rochioli and Allen vineyards are all about finesse, leaner with higher acidity and more purity of line.

Jordan Vineyard & Winery *

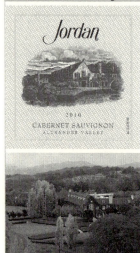

 1474 Alexander Road, Healdsburg, CA 95448
 (1) 800 654 1213
 Lisa Mattson
 info@jordanwinery.com
 www.jordanwinery.com
 Alexander Valley
 Cabernet Sauvignon

111 acres; 1,200,000 bottles
[map p. 112]

Jordan has followed an unusual course of development, moving from 100% Estate wine in 1990 to 2% today. "Tom Jordan wanted to make wine in the style of Bordeaux. He thought that what separated the first growths was that they owned their own vineyards, but the tenor of the time was that soil wasn't important, you just put in the right cultivar for the degree days," says winemaker Rob Davis, who has been in charge of every vintage since the inaugural 1976. Phylloxera forced replanting after 1990, but many of the vineyard blocks have been abandoned or the grapes sold off. Today most (80%) of the fruit for Jordan's wines comes from around twenty growers, many located in Geyserville.

The Jordan Cabernet Sauvignon is usually at the limit for varietal labeling (75% Cabernet Sauvignon), with Merlot as the second component, and then about 4-7% Petit Verdot and 1% Malbec. A mixture of French and American oak is used for maturation. The wines are intended to be drinkable on release—an important aspect being that Jordan has a major presence in restaurants—and the style is best described by Rob Davis: "I like fruit," but these tend to elegance rather than power, and there's a firm policy of keeping to moderate alcohol levels (recent vintages are all stated at 13.5%). The wines seem to alternate between richer, heavier vintages in New World style (2008, 2006, 2003) and more elegant vintages in more European style (2007, 2004, 1990).

Joseph Swan Vineyards *

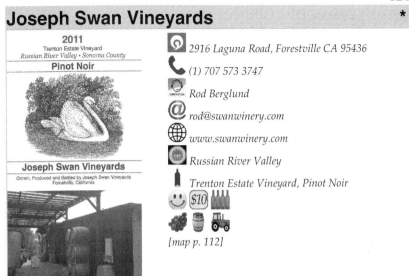

2916 Laguna Road, Forestville CA 95436

(1) 707 573 3747

Rod Berglund

rod@swanwinery.com

www.swanwinery.com

Russian River Valley

Trenton Estate Vineyard, Pinot Noir

$10

[map p. 112]

While he was working as an airline pilot, Joseph Swan started his vineyard by purchasing a small farm in Russian River Valley in 1967. There was some Zinfandel on the farm, but he began replanting the vineyard to Pinot Noir, Chardonnay and Cabernet Sauvignon in 1968. The first vintage of the Pinot Noir was 1973. Rod Berglund joined the winery in 1979, and runs it today together with his wife Lynn, Joe Swan's daughter. Rod was part of a group of winemakers who tried to define the typicity of Pinot Noir in Russian River Valley. It was perhaps too early because they did not reach agreement, he explains. "Swan produces Pinot Noir from several sites all of which are different. I think site triumphs all else. I like working with a multiplicity of clones because that gives a more complex wine," he says.

The winery remains focused on Pinot Noir; its proportion of production varies with the year, but is usually around 50-60%. The original selection of Pinot Noir was from Mt. Eden, but it did so well that in due course it became known as the Swan clone. Although the Swan selection of Pinot Noir is a famous clone in California, Joe Swan began grafting over to Dijon clones (or other selections from Burgundy), because he thought they gave better results. There are four bottlings of Pinot Noir; one comes from estate fruit and is matured in three quarters new oak, the others are matured in one third new oak. The Trenton Station Vineyard is part of the estate and makes a rather Burgundian Pinot Noir.

Kamen Wines

111B East Napa Street, Sonoma CA 95476

(1) 707 938 7292

Robert Kamen

info@kamenwines.com

www.kamenwines.com

Sonoma Valley

Moon Mountain Cabernet Sauvignon

$20

46 acres; 42,000 bottles

[map p. 112]

Perched on the top of Moon Mountain, Kamen is idiosyncratic. Visits start at the tasting room in downtown Sonoma, then you go in a four wheel drive SUV to the vineyards up a steep, winding track on to the mountain, where Robert Kamen has a small house. Some of the vineyards are accessible only in an off-road vehicle.

Robert was a professor at the University of Pennsylvania, who turned a novel into a screen play in 1979 (he then became a screenwriter), and used the proceeds to buy the estate on the advice of his friend Phil Coturri, a well known viticulturalist. "This guy took me up here, it was 1,000 acres and I bought it with $135,000," he says. Extending over 300 acres, from 1,400 to 2,200 feet, it has views over San Pablo Bay to San Francisco in the distance.

There are about 13 different vineyard plots on the estate, which focuses on Cabernet Sauvignon. Soils are volcanic, with blocks of basalt everywhere. The estate Cabernet Sauvignon is about two thirds of production; in addition Kashmir is made only in exceptional vintages—"which means drought years here"—and Lava Block has been introduced as a single vineyard designate. The style is rich and forceful, with strong black and blue fruit aromatics, but the texture is very fine and the tannins are refined, very sleek rather than giving an impression of mountain tannins. Kashmir is less obvious, with an even more refined texture. New oak is 65% for the estate and 100% for Kashmir.

The wines are now labeled under the Moon Mountain District AVA, which Robert was instrumental in creating. "The whole point of doing the AVA was that I got tired of making wines that are completely different from everything else, I got tired of explaining to people that we are not typical Sonoma County, with the attitude that average is okay."

Kistler Vineyards ★

4707 Vine Hill Road, Sebastopol CA 95472

(1) 707 823 5603

Steve Kistler

info@kistlervineyards.com

www.kistlervineyards.com

Russian River Valley

Sonoma County, Les Noisetiers, Chardonnay

$75

420,000 bottles

[map p. 112]

Steve Kistler and Marc Bixler met in 1974 and started the winery in 1979. "We are still doing it, which is not really true of most startup wineries. Usually the principals have either changed or they have hired other people to do the work," said Marc, who died in 2017. Steve Kistler continues as the winemaker.

Kistler makes wine from two different areas. There are several vineyards within 4 miles of the rather discrete winery which is identified only by the road number. The home vineyard is all Chardonnay. The main Pinot Noir vineyards are about a mile or so north and south of the winery. Most are labeled as Sonoma Coast even if they are Russian River Valley.

Many of their old vineyard bottlings were from grapes purchased from specific vineyards, but now they own all their own vineyards. "It's so difficult to grow we don't want to rely on others. Our style of Pinot Noir over rides regional specificities. We have a very specific style and it affects the methods we use. We want a very richly flavored style without too strong tannin influence. We don't do anything to eliminate tannins," said Marc.

A change in tannin management really occurred in 2002, although there was a transition from 1999-2001. The change has made the wines easier to drink sooner, although that wasn't the major objective. New oak has been reduced from 100% to 80%. If anything, Kistler is better known for its Chardonnays—there are about 12 different Chardonnays compared to 5 Pinots—mostly from single vineyards. The blended wines are really a sort of second label to the single vineyard wines. Marc summarized the style: "Kistler should have a powerful nose with fruit, some oak but not too noticeable, a great deal of rich fruit in the mouth with lots of dark flavors, ripe but fresh not jammy or muddy."

Kosta Browne Winery **

1300 Montgomery Road, Sebastopol CA 95472

(1) 707 823 7430

Tony Lombardi

kb@kostabrowne.com

www.kostabrowne.com

Russian River Valley

Russian River Valley, Keefer, Pinot Noir

300,000 bottles

[map p. 112]

Kosta Browne began when Dan Kosta and Michael Browne, who were in the restaurant business, started by buying grapes and a barrel and made some wine. From one barrel (about 25 cases) they moved to 250 cases and then to 2,500 cases. They raised capital in 2001 and became professional. All their grapes are purchased. Kosta Browne is located in an old facility that used to be a center for handling apples in Sonoma. Venture capital firm Vincraft (who subsequently bought Gary Farrell) bought a controlling stake in 2009, and in turn sold it to a Boston group in 2015.

Other producers often refer to Kosta Browne wines as 'big.' "We got typecast into being this super-extracted Pinot Noir," says Dan Kosta. This actually happened as an accident, when some fruit came in at very high (25.2) Brix. "We made the wine, and it was just perfectly exhilarating. That turned me on to picking fruit when it tasted good, rather than when people are telling me," Dan says.

The wines are high in alcohol and extract, and represent the forceful Californian style. But I can't say they necessarily appear over the top to me, as tasting barrel samples from different clones, oak, or means of vinification shows an interesting range of differences. The wines are certainly forceful, but have balanced smooth palates emphasizing the fruits. Alcohol usually pushes close to 15%, which may be a problem in matching foods, and the supple tannins are subsumed by the fruits. These may well be wines to consume relatively early rather than to age.

Dan Kosta and Michael Browne stayed on, but left in 2017 to make wines at a new venture, Cirq, where interestingly there is less extract and lower alcohol. Looking back, "We got typecast into being this super-extracted Pinot Noir," says Dan Kosta, "People trying to make a restrained style would use us as an example of what they *didn't* want to do." A more restrained style may also be seen in the future under the new regime at Kosta Browne.

Littorai Wines *

788 Gold Ridge Rd, Sebastopol, CA 95472
(1) 707 823 9586
Maureen Flaherty
info@littorai.com
www.littorai.com
Russian River Valley
Sonoma Coast, Hirsch Vineyard, Pinot Noir
$40
44 acres; 72,000 bottles
[map p. 112]

Ted Lemon began Littorai in 1993 with just 300 cases of production. "When we started I did not have any interest in what I think of as the American flamboyant school of wine," he says, so the target was to sell to restaurants where a more elegant style might be better received. This now accounts for roughly two thirds of sales, the rest going to a mailing list. About 40% of production comes from estate vineyards, owned or on long term lease, the rest from purchased fruit. The estate vineyards stretch from the winery at the western edge of Russian River Valley to the Anderson Valley.

Ted is an enthusiast for biodynamic viticulture. "We rejected organic viticulture because it substituted organic for synthetic but retained the basic idea of western agronomy," he says, adding that this is not so true of organic viticulture today. Littorai started to go biodynamic in 1998. Consisting of 12 hectares of farmland with about 10% planted to a Pinot Noir vineyard, the home estate will ultimately become completely self sufficient; all it lacks at the moment is a cow. Winemaking is as natural as possible, a major target being to avoid acidification. New oak is usually around 30% except for the two blended Pinots that are about 10%. The wines have an unusual elegance for the region.

Martinelli Winery & Vineyards *

3360 River Road, Windsor, CA 95492

(1) 707 525 0570

vinoinfo@martinelliwinery.com

www.martinelliwinery.com

Russian River Valley

Russian River Valley, Jackas Vineyard Zinfandel

$25

400 acres; 132,000 bottles

[map p. 112]

The Martinellis originally came from Italy as a young married couple in the late 1880s. The fifth generation is now running Martinelli. They are still farming the original vineyard that Giuseppe planted on Jackass Hill. There are eighteen vineyards all over Russian River Valley, and another six at Fort Ross-Seaview. The Martinellis are really growers rather than winemakers, as they sell 90% of production and make wine only from the remaining 10%.

There are about 30 different cuvées from Chardonnay, Pinot Noir, Zinfandel, and Syrah (relatively small production), but the focus is on Pinot Noir and Zinfandel. All of the wines are monovarietals. In terms of sources, there is one blended Chardonnay, two blended Pinot Noirs, and one blended Zinfandel: everything else is a single vineyard.

The style of the Chardonnays varies with the vineyard, but there's a tendency to a richer style showing tropical fruits. Pinot Noirs vary from the stern palate of Bondi Home Ranch coming from the cool Green River to the voluptuous soft aromatics of Russian River proper, but the latter is more typical.

Zinfandels are in the full force style, with high alcohol (16% or more), powerful aromatics with hints of piquancy, and Port-like impressions. The top Zinfandel is Jackass Hill, which was planted by Giuseppe and has 120 year-old vines, but Jackass Vineyard, already planted when Giuseppe bought the property, is close to it with 135-140 year-old vines planted at the bottom of the hill. The Vigneto di Evo Zinfandel from Russian River, which has typical high-toned aromatics, is the most popular wine in the tasting room.

The first Syrah from the Martinelli vineyards was made by Helen Turley, and the style still shows it: super-ripe to over-ripe, with punishing alcohol well over 16%. It may be fair to say the Syrahs are for people who would like Zinfandel with a bit of structure. If there is a single word to describe Martinelli's style, it would be voluptuous.

Matanzas Creek Winery

6097 Bennett Valley Road, Santa Rosa, CA 95404
(1) 800 590 6464
info@matanzascreek.com
www.matanzascreek.com
Russian River Valley

Sonoma County, Journey, Sauvignon Blanc

$15

440,000 bottles

[map p. 112]

Matanzas Creek was there right at the start of the revival of winemaking on the North Coast, when it was established in 1977 in Bennett Valley to the east of Santa Rosa (long before Bennett Valley became an AVA). The location is a little off the beaten winery track in Sonoma. Originally a family winery, with wines made in an old barn, the property changed hands in 2000 when it was bought by Kendall-Jackson. Winemaking was moved to Jackson's larger facility at Stonestreet in 2010 to allow renovations at Matanzas Creek, and Marcia Monahan-Torres became the winemaker.

There are varietal wines from Chardonnay, Sauvignon Blanc, and Merlot. Journey is used as the label for the top wines, and includes the same varietals as well as a blended red. There are several Sauvignon Blancs from different locations, two Chardonnays, and four bottlings of Merlot. Differences between the bottlings are carefully cultivated—Marcia selects yeasts for fermentation according to the property of each batch of grapes, for example—but Journey is more complete and complex in each case.

Merry Edwards Wines ✱✱

830 Denbe Saint Court, Suite B, Windsor, CA 95492

(1) 707 823 7466

Lindsay Joule

merry@merryedwards.com

www.merryedwards.com

Russian River Valley

Russian River Valley, Olivet Lane, Pinot Noir

275,000 bottles

[map p. 112]

Merry Edwards is regarded as one of the pioneer winemakers in California. Her interest in Pinot Noir dates from her first winemaking position in 1974 at Mount Eden Vineyards in the Santa Cruz Mountains. From the plantings there she developed the Rae clone (now known as UCD 37), which is a major part of her own estate. As a Chardonnay specialist, she was the founding winemaker at Matanzas Creek in 1977. Her own winery was founded in 1997.

Wines come from six estate vineyards and also from two vineyards under long-term acreage contracts allowing her to control viticulture. "We feel that farming is the only way to come to great Pinot and that is what we have based everything on," she says. In addition to the single vineyard wines, there is a Russian River bottling consisting of declassified lots. The Sonoma Coast bottling, which was made from purchased fruit, was discontinued. The Sauvignon Blanc is barrel fermented in the style of Fumé Blanc.

Vinification for Pinot Noir follows the usual lines, although there's a little more use of new oak than average, running to around 55-60% in the regional blends and to 75-80% in the single vineyard designations. Describing her wines, she says, "I probably have two stylistic aims. I like the fruit to come through, I view this as the personality of the wine. And I like to see the texture come through."

Patz & Hall Wine Co. **

21200 8th St E, Sonoma, CA 95476
(1) 707 265 7700
James Hall
info@patzhall.com
www.patzhall.com
Sonoma Valley
Carneros, Hyde Vineyard Pinot Noir
Sonoma Coast Chardonnay
$35
0 acres; 600,000 bottles   [map p. 112]

"I concocted this crazy plan with Donald Patz to make Chardonnay. At that time Chardonnay was the cash flow white—blended wine made by Cabernet winemakers—but Donald and I were very interested in Burgundy; comprising a wine on the blending table was not Burgundian at all, and we thought there was an opportunity to make single vineyard wines in California," recalls James Hall. The first two vintages were difficult, but the third, in 1990, came from the Hyde Vineyard in Carneros and was an instant success. From 1998 to 2007 the wine was made at Honig where James was the winemaker, but since then has been made at a purpose-built facility that James designed. The tasting room is just down the road, converted from a former residence.

Today there are 22 cuvées. Three wines are available for national distribution, the Sonoma Coast Chardonnay and Pinot Noir, and Dutton Ranch Chardonnay; everything else is under 1,000 cases. Is Burgundy still the inspiration? "It is for winemaking and for having a relationship with a vineyard block, as opposed to a Bordeaux philosophy, but we are not trying to make Burgundy. These wines do not taste anything like Burgundy but I do admire their process, that's the important takeaway," James says. "Winemaking is similar for all wines, one of my philosophies is to standardize the winemaking to let terroir differences show." Alcohol is more or less steady around 13.9-14.2%. "We generally pick around 23 Brix, I'm very interested preserving natural acidity."

The Sonoma Coast wines show the house style but there's more individual character from the single vineyards, becoming more generous or more reserved depending on the vineyard. The Sonoma Coast Chardonnay is rich and delicious, but the Hyde Vineyard from Carneros is less obvious, with more minerality in the background, and the Ritchie Vineyard from Russian River takes longer to come out of its shell. The Sonoma Coast Pinot is quite reserved for the new world, Gap's Crown Vineyard (which looks down on the Petaluma Gap) moves in a herbal direction, but Hyde Vineyard from Carneros is supple, rounder, and more unctuous. "I refuse to adjust wines for immediate consumption, I still insist on making some wines that are smoky and reduced and need to age," James says, but most are ready to start within a year or so of release.

Paul Hobbs Winery **

3355 Gravenstein Hwy North, Sebastopol CA 95472

(1) 707 824 9879

Paul Hobbs

concierge@paulhobbs.com

www.paulhobbswinery.com

Sonoma Valley

Russian River Valley, Pinot Noir

Napa Valley, Cabernet Sauvignon

Russian River Valley, Chardonnay

$65

207 acres; 300,000 bottles [map p. 112]

"I've always liked living on the edge," says Paul Hobbs, who now makes wine not only in California, but also in Mendoza, Cahors, Armenia, and the Finger Lakes. Under the name of the Paul Hobbs winery, he produces all three major varietals from Sonoma and Napa. The focus is on single vineyard wines, although Paul prefers the term vineyard designates. There is one general appellation wine for each variety, and a large number of single vineyard wines, about 27 at last count, although Paul is still acquiring new vineyards, and new wines are constantly being added. Cabernet Sauvignon is about 40% of production, and Pinot Noir and Chardonnay are about 30% each.

Sources depend on the variety: "I want to focus on the highest and best regions in Sonoma Coast, including Russian River, but for Cabernet there's no question but that Napa is the place to be." Within a year or so, all of the Pinot Noir and Chardonnay will comes from estate grapes, but the Cabernet mostly comes from grapes purchased from top vineyards. Stylistic objectives are deceptively simple. "Nothing has changed since I started. I want to have a clear sense of place. We only use native yeast, there is no fining, no filtration. We only pick at night so grapes are cool, and everything is hand harvested."

Chardonnay comes from four vineyards in Russian River and one on Sonoma Mountain, Pinot Noir comes from three vineyards in Russian River, one on Sonoma Mountain, and the Hyde vineyard in Carneros. Cabernet comes from three Beckstoffer vineyards in Napa, including To-Kalon, and the Nathan Coombs estate in Coombsville (recently acquired and the source of estate grapes). The style is powerful but not overwhelming. The richness of Chardonnay tends to be cut by faint herbal impressions, the Pinot Noir is smooth and unctuous, and Cabernet varies from the (relative) restraint of Nathan Coombs to the more aromatic impressions of the Napa cuvées.

In addition to the Paul Hobbs label, there is also Cross Barn, which depends exclusively on purchased grapes, and focuses on appellations rather than single vineyards: the style is similar but not so precise. Viña Cobos in Mendoza is Paul's venture in Argentina, and is the largest of the wineries. Cross Barn is about twice the size of Paul Hobbs, which is actually the smallest of three major enterprises. The latest venture in Finger Lakes is a tribute to Paul's origins in upstate New York (but not to his background in a teetotal family).

Peter Michael ★★

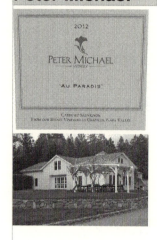

12400 Ida Clayton Road, Calistoga, CA 94515

(1) 707 942 3200

Peter Kay

retail@petermichaelwinery.com

www.petermichaelwinery.com

Knights Valley

Sonoma Coast, Le Caprice Pinot Noir

Knights Valley, Les Pavots Proprietary Red

Knights Valley, La Carrière Chardonnay

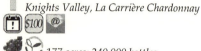

177 acres; 240,000 bottles

[map p. 112]

Located about an hour north of Napa, although the address says Calistoga, the Peter Michael Winery is in Knight's Valley of Sonoma County. The winery dates from the purchase of 630 acres of volcanic terrain on the slopes of Mount St. Helena in 1982. "This was a retired cattle ranch with no habitable buildings when we bought it," says manager Peter Kay. You can drive a long way around the estate before you see the vineyards, which are tucked into the forest. "The unusual feature of this property is that we can grow Cabernet which requires heat, and Chardonnay which needs cooler temperatures, only 500 yards apart, because there is a gap that channels marine air into the cooler area, whereas the other areas are protected. The difference in temperature is 4-8 degrees," Peter explains. The homestead house that provides the tasting room is at about 500 foot elevation, and vineyards go up to 2,000 feet. The winery is housed in a series of buildings close by, with separate facilities for each variety.

The flagship wine is the Bordeaux Blend, Les Pavots, (typically about two thirds Cabernet Sauvignon), with a second wine l'Esprit des Pavots coming from younger vines. There are four Chardonnays from different vineyards on the Knights Valley estate, and a Bordeaux white blend, l'Après Midi. Pinot Noirs all come from an estate purchased in Fort Ross-Seaview in Sonoma County in 1998. The Cabernet Au Paradis comes from a vineyard that was recently purchased in Oakville, marking the winery's first venture into Napa ("the first time we have bought a vineyard as opposed to developing one from scratch"). Available only by subscription, with a waiting list, the wines have a fine reputation for understated elegance, but for my palate the power of the New World is evident.

With alcohol levels of 14.5-15%, the Chardonnays make a powerful impression, with a viscous palate rich in stone fruits. The Sauvignon Blanc is one of the richest in the Fumé Blanc style. The Pinot Noirs show minerality and delicate floral impressions, but still have the fat of California. The Bordeaux blends are the pièce de résistance, with Les Pavots showing purity of fruits with some high-toned impressions against a viscous background, and Au Paradis showing the tightness and power of Oakville. Use of oak is restrained: "In our portfolio there is nothing with 100% new oak, our style is for the oak to be integrated, with elegance and natural acidity," says winemaker Nick Morlet, who comes from Champagne. "This winery is Californian, but the owner is British, and the names of the wines are French, so we need French sensitivity," he adds. Yet these are cult wines, with the power of California always evident.

Ramey Wine Cellars

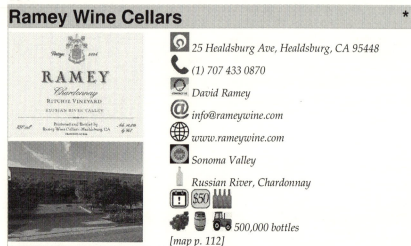

25 Healdsburg Ave, Healdsburg, CA 95448
(1) 707 433 0870
David Ramey
info@rameywine.com
www.rameywine.com
Sonoma Valley
Russian River, Chardonnay
$50
500,000 bottles
[map p. 112]

David Ramey founded his own cellar in 1996 after making wines for several wineries in Sonoma and Napa. Most of the vineyards are in Russian River, and this is the basis for several single vineyard Chardonnays, which together with the Russian River Valley and Sonoma Coast bottlings are a major focus. There are also Pinot Noirs and Syrahs from Sonoma, and Cabernet Sauvignon from Napa. A second label called Sidebar, introducing cheaper wines in a lighter style, was added in 2015.

The Ramey Chardonnays typify a more restrained Sonoma style (compared with the greater exuberance of Napa); the general Sonoma bottlings show more obvious evidence of oak than the single vineyards, where Ritchie Vineyard is the most subtle, and Hyde vineyard is more exotic and assertive. The Russian River Valley is a nice compromise. Among the reds I especially like Pedregal Vineyard Cabernet Sauvignon for its sense of precision. East-facing Rogers Creek vineyard in Sonoma produces a restrained Syrah along European lines; the west-facing Shanel vineyard produces more of a full-force New World expression of Syrah.

Ridge Vineyards (Lytton Springs) **

RIDGE 2008
CALIFORNIA
ZINFANDEL
PONZO
VINEYARD

98% ZINFANDEL, 2% PETITE SIRAH
RUSSIAN RIVER VALLEY 15.1% ALCOHOL BY VOLUME
PRODUCED AND BOTTLED BY RIDGE VINEYARDS
650 LYTTON SPRINGS ROAD, HEALDSBURG, CALIFORNIA 95448

650 Lytton Springs Road, Healdsburg, CA 95448, USA

(1) 707 431 2634

John Olney

reservations@ridgewine.com

www.ridgewine.com

Russian River Valley

① Alexander Valley, Geyserville Zinfandel

② Sonoma County, Three Valleys Zinfandel

$10

429 acres; 480,000 bottles [map p. 112]

"Ridge started making single vineyard Zins in the 1960s—no one else was doing this," says winemaker John Olney. Ridge's first commitment was to producing Bordeaux blends in Santa Cruz (see profile of Ridge Vineyards), but Paul Draper decided very early to express other varieties as well. The objective was to identify vineyards with unique characters. The oldest of today's cuvées is Geyserville, which Ridge first produced in 1966. The first Zinfandel from Lytton Springs was produced in 1972; the vineyards were purchased in 1991, and the winery was constructed in 1999.

Today Ridge at Lytton Springs produces Zinfandels from the Lytton Springs vineyard besides the winery, the larger Lytton Ranch just beyond, the famous vineyard in Geyserville in the next valley to the north, and Ponzo vineyard in Russian River. All of these are single vineyard wines, all part of the estate except for Ponzo where the grapes are purchased; in addition, the Three Valleys Zinfandel is basically a second wine from declassified lots.

Lytton Springs and Geyserville are old vineyards, planted with field blends a century ago. "Zinfandel's weakness is that it loves the sun but makes a lot of sugar," says John Olney, "so if you have a field blend with other varieties, overall there is less sugar and more elegance." The other varieties are mostly Carignan and Petite Syrah. This partly explains the style, which tends towards silky elegance, with aromatics nicely restrained, and hints of structure in the background, without the forced exuberance of high alcohol. Another factor is that alcohol levels are moderate. "We usually pick early, often ten days earlier than anyone else," John explains. Paul Draper experimented in the nineties and decided that he preferred American oak, so this is now used for all wines.

The cuvées are distinctive: Geyserville is the most forward and ready to drink, with more uplifted aromatics; Ponzo is a more restrained style representing Russian River; Lytton Springs is the most structured, tight on release and needing a year or so. The differences are partly due to the blend of varieties in each vineyard, and partly due to climatic differences, with Russian River relatively cool, and Lytton Springs not as warm as Geyserville.

Rochioli Vineyards & Winery *

6192 Westside Rd, Healdsburg, CA 95448

(1) 707 433 2305

Tom Rochioli

info@rochioliwinery.com

www.rochioliwinery.com

Russian River Valley

Sonoma County, Pinot Noir

$20

150 acres; 144,000 bottles

[map p. 112]

Rochioli is one of the most famous names in Russian River, with several vineyards on the estate where grapes are bought by top producers to make single-vineyard releases. A family of immigrants from Italy with an agricultural background, the Rochiolis were farming in Sonoma and in 1934 they moved to what became the Rochioli estate when they were able to purchase the land in the 1950s. In 1958 Joe Rochioli asked the University of Davis for advice on what would be the most appropriate crops. The University recommended grapes, but early attempts with Cabernet Sauvignon and Sauvignon Blanc were not entirely successful. The first Pinot Noir was planted in 1968, and Chardonnay followed soon after. Grapes were sold to wineries specializing in Pinot Noir—Davis Bynum were one of the first—and the various vineyards at the estate became known through these bottlings. Rochioli farm the vineyards, but purchasers can decide when they want to harvest. (There can be conflicts: one year Gary Farrell had to wait a day, because Williams Selyem got there first and the pickers were engaged.)

Today about 60% of the grapes are sold but only some of the purchasers are allowed to use the Rochioli name on the label: Williams Selyem, Gary Farrell, and Long Board. Others buy the grapes but cannot use the name; it's part of the agreement that Rochioli tastes the wine, with right to approve or deny use of the name annually. Rochioli started making their own wine with the 1985 vintage. Today's range includes Pinot Noir (4,000 cases), Sauvignon Blanc (4,000 cases), and Chardonnay (2,500 cases). In addition to general estates wines, for the mailing list only there are four Chardonnays and four Pinot Noirs from single vineyards (3-Corners, Little hill, East block, and West block), most produced in 100-200 case lots. The principle here is minimal manipulation. All wines use one third new, one third one-year, and one third 2 two-year oak. The style is fruit-driven and relatively robust.

Rodney Strong Vineyards **

11455 Old Redwood Highway, Healdsburg, CA 95448

(1) 707 433 6521

Rick Sayre

info@rodneystrong.com

www.rodneystrong.com

Russian River Valley

Russian River Valley Pinot Noir

Alexander Valley, Symmetry Meritage

Chalk Hill Chardonnay

 1580 acres; 950,000 bottles

[map p. 112]

Rodney Strong is a significant vineyard in the history of Sonoma. Rodney was in fact a very successful ballet dancer who turned to wine. He first set up shop in the yacht club at Tiburon and sold wines that he blended to the wealthy clientele. He did so well in the first couple of years that he was able to buy land in Russian River and establish the winery. He was a visionary, but not so successful as a businessman and went bankrupt twice. Rodney Strong winery was sold to the Klein family in 1989, who have built it up to its present position. Behind the snazzy tasting room just off the highway, there is a vast operation with multiple wineries. Each has its own approach, from the "artisan winery" with 73 small tanks of varying sizes to the new winery just constructed to take grapes from a new vineyard purchase, which is packed with 57 identical square tanks.

Wines are divided into three tiers. The Sonoma County tier includes Cabernet, Chardonnay, and Merlot, and accounts for two thirds of production. The 30% in the Estate tier includes eight wines: Sauvignon Blanc, two Chardonnay, two Pinot Noir, Zinfandel, two Cabernet Sauvignon. The Reserve wines are only about 5% and include eight small production wines sold only at the winery or to the wine club. Winemaker Justin Seidenfeld came from Mondavi in 2010. When asked to define house style, he says, "The uniform thread of house style is that place matters. Differences in vinification are intended to bring out the character of place. I did trials on winemaking to find out what would best show vineyard character based on my understanding of the vineyard."

There is a variety of styles here. "The Chalk Hill Chardonnay is barrel fermented with full MLF, monthly battonage, and 30% new oak. The Sonoma Coast Chardonnay comes from a vineyard in the Petaluma gap and is half barrel fermented, half fermented in stainless steel barrels; the wood half gets MLF, the half does not." Chalk Hill shows classic impressions of oak with buttery overtones; Sonoma Coast is much leaner and more citrus driven. The styles are based on Justin's view that

Chalk Hill is suited to make more traditional wines, Sonoma Coast more modern wines.

Symmetry is the top blended wine. "It's our version of the best wine we can make from the vintage irrespective of variety. The blend differs every vintages." A Meritage, this is quite Bordelais, with a balance in which the structure is subservient to restrained fruits. The peak of Cabernet expression comes from three single vineyard wines from Alexander Valley: all show a fine texture with an elegant expression of black fruits, more structured for the pure varietals of Alexander's Crown and Brothers, a little broader for Rockaway which includes the other Bordeaux varieties. "Those are the best places, but they are all different. That's why they are the best," Justin says.

Treasury Wine Estates

Sbragia Family Vineyards ★★

9990 Dry Creek Road, Geyserville, California 95441

(1) 707 473 2992

Steve Cousins

info@sbragia.com

www.sbragia.com

Sonoma Valley

Andolsen Vineyard, Cabernet Sauvignon

$20

49 acres; 150,000 bottles

[map p. 112]

Ed Sbragia grew up in Dry Creek Valley—"basically my heritage is Zinfandel and French Colombard," he says—got a chemistry degree from Davis, worked for Gallo, discovered wine, went back to school, worked for Foppiano for a year, and then went to Beringer for 32 years. He started his own production in 2001, while still at Beringer. His first release was in 2004. He purchased his present property in 2006. His own grapes are Sauvignon Blanc, Zinfandel, Chardonnay, Merlot; purchased grapes come from growers in Dry Creek and in Mayacamas mountains, and from two vineyards on Howell Mountain.

All the Cabernets are single vineyard designates, with about 10 tons of grapes making 250 cases each. His son is the winemaker. The Sbragia winery is located in Sonoma, but most of his Cabernets come from Napa. Tasting here is especially interesting as the wines are all distinct, and it is an opportunity to see if there is any consistent difference between wines made by the same winemaker on the Napa side versus those from the Sonoma side of the Mayacamas mountains.

Kendall-Jackson

Stonestreet *

7111 Highway 128, Healdsburg, CA 95448 (winery),
337 Healdsburg Ave,

(1) 707 433 9469

Kelly Keagy

info@stonestreetwines.com

www.stonestreetwines.com

Alexander Valley

Monument Ridge, Cabernet Sauvignon

$15

185 acres; 40,000 bottles
[map p. 112]

Stonestreet was created by Jesse Jackson, who started in wine by purchasing an orchard of pear and walnut trees in Lakeport (in the Central Valley) and converting it to a vineyard for Chardonnay production. He purchased a mountain estate in Sonoma's Alexander Valley in 1995 and turned it into a brand for Cabernet Sauvignon and Chardonnay. (Stonestreet was his middle name.)

Stonestreet has 3,200 ha with 350 ha planted, including 200 ha of Cabernet Sauvignon. The vineyards are largely on the mountain slopes, where 80 ha had been planted in 1982, another 80 ha in 1991, more by Jackson after the acquisition in 1995, and then again in 2005. The overall balance of production is 80% red.

Stonestreet is part of Jackson Family Vineyards, and while some of the grapes are used for its own bottlings, some are used by other vineyards in the group. The Stonestreet facility is also used to make wine for other properties in the group. The Stonestreet facility is also used to make wine for other properties in the group. It's possible to taste either at the winery or at the tasting room in downtown Healdsburg.

Cabernet tends to be grown on higher plots on the mountains, because an inversion layer of cold air lower down makes ripening difficult. A series of monovarietal Cabernet Sauvignons come from single vineyards, Bear Point (below the fog line at 1.200 foot), West Ledge (within the fog line at 1,800 foot), and Monolith and Christopher (above the fog line at 2,100 foot and 2,400 foot). Monument Ridge is a bottling from sites all across the property. Legacy is an Alexander Valley blend that includes lots from the valley floor. "Mountain sites give far more variability in growth and ripening than on the flat. New plantings of Merlot, Petit Verdot, and Malbec are going very well; but blending them in would cause loss of site specificity," says winemaker Graham Weerts. The Stonestreet wines are not wines for immediate gratification, which has been a marketing problem in the past. Recent efforts have focused on trying to make the wines a little rounder and more opulent.

Vérité

4611 Thomas Road, Healdsburg, CA 95448
(1) 707 433 9000
Pierre Seillan
info@veritewines.com
www.veritewines.com
Sonoma Valley
$150

[map p. 112]

"We met Jess and Barbara Jackson in the mid nineties, came here for a short experiment—and we are still here," Monique Seillan recalls. Vérité started when Jess asked Pierre Seillan to make a top Merlot blend. Originally it was just called Vérité, but when more cuvées were introduced, it became Vérité La Muse. La Joie is a blend based on Cabernet Sauvignon, and Le Désir is a blend based on Cabernet Franc. All the Vérité wines are blends from a variety of sources in different valleys of Sonoma, each being based on the major variety, comprising from 60% to 85%, with the rest coming from other Bordeaux varieties. "Pierre believes there are many differences even in one vineyard and vinifies many micro crus separately before deciding how to blend," Monique explains. As a result the wines have only the lowly appellation of Sonoma County.

The Vérité wines are made at the functional-looking winery a few miles east of Healdsburg. Pierre also makes the wines for Anakota, a separate brand, at the Vérité winery, but visits to Anakota are made to a tasting room in Calistoga (the address is revealed only after an appointment has been made). Anakota produces two monovarietal Cabernet Sauvignons from the Helena Montana and Helena Dakota vineyards in Knights Valley, just south of the Peter Michael winery. "It is very rare for Pierre to make a single vineyard wine, Anakota is the only one he does," Monique says. These are made in very small amounts, about 400 cases each. All the Vérité and Anakota wines see 100% new oak. Alcohol is not outrageous, typically in the mid 14s, as Pierre picks early.

Intensity is the most appropriate single word to describe the style. Dense fruits are not exuberant or jammy, but so intense that tannins are pushed back, and it would be possible to drink straight away. Of course, this would be a pity, as the wines develop very slowly, and it takes at least ten years before the flavor variety begins to broaden out, when they tend to move in the direction of minerality. La Muse gives the most forward fruits and most supple tannic impression, La Joie has the finest texture making the tannins less obvious, and Le Désir has that velvety sense of a chocolaty texture that comes from Cabernet Franc at its ripest. Each of the Vérité wines shows the typicity of its predominant variety through the blend.

The Anakota wines have the more direct quality of pure Cabernet Sauvignon, with Helena Dakota the finest, and Helena Montana restrained by more powerful mountain tannins. The Seillans have an impressive range; Pierre also makes wine in Chianti Classico and partners the Jacksons in making a grand cru St. Emilion, Château Lassegue.

Walter Hansel

5465 Hall Rd, Santa Rosa, CA 95401
(1) 707 525 3614
Stephen Hansel
shansel@hanselwine.com
www.walterhanselwinery.com
Russian River Valley
Russian River Valley, The Meadow Chardonnay
79 acres; 114,000 bottles
[map p. 112]

"I purposely made it like this," says Stephen Hansel, gesturing to the barebones warehouse behind the crush pad where he had set up a table for tasting, "because it's about the wine and the wine doesn't care about fancy buildings." This is a small operation with only six full time employees who are involved in everything from viticulture to vinification. The winery is right in the middle of the vineyard, which is not the most obvious terrain for wine as it's partly in a flood plain and the soils are quite fertile. Yet some of the most Burgundian Chardonnays and Pinot Noirs of Russian River come from here. Aside from a Sauvignon Blanc from a vineyard in Lake County, all production is from the home vineyard.

"We make five Chardonnays and five Pinot Noirs. The differences between them are mostly in the clones—the Estate Chardonnay is an exception from multiple clones—my interest is not in intervention, I'm more interested in showing what the clones can do, we have 80 acres here, how much terroir difference can there be?" Stephen says. Burgundy has always been his bench mark; discussion of the cuvées is peppered with references to white or red Burgundy.

The Estate Chardonnay is in a relatively rich style, whereas The Meadows (all Hanzell clone) shows more minerality. Three Rows, 100% Pommard clone, is one of the most Burgundian, with a silky delicacy reminiscent of Chambolle Musigny, while North Slope is richer. "This is clone 115 and has always been a Californian wine, but that's okay, I want each one of my wines to be different, otherwise I could put them all in the same bottle." The house style tends to a silky smoothness, with just a touch of fat on the palate to remind you that the wines come from California; the impression of a European aesthetic is reinforced by alcohol levels, which are moderate for the region at or just over 14%.

Williams Selyem **

7227 Westside Road, Healdsburg, CA 95448

(1) 707 433 6425

Jeff Mangahas

contact@williamsselyem.com

www.williamsselyem.com

Russian River Valley

Russian River, Allen Vineyard Pinot Noir

101 acres; 250,000 bottles

[map p. 112]

Williams Selyem is one of the standard bearers for Russian River Valley, and one of the original pioneers still remaining independent. Started by Ed Selyem and Burt Williams, who had been amateur winemakers, the first vintage was made in a two-car garage in 1981; the original name of Hacienda del Rio was changed to Williams Selyem in 1984. Burt Williams made the vintages through 1997, when the winery was sold to John and Kathe Dyson, after which Bob Cabral took over as winemaker, making all the wines until 2013. Jeff Mangahas worked with Bob for two years before taking over. "My inspiration for coming here was the wines that Burt made in the early days," he says. Production functioned out of what was virtually a trailer park until 2010, when a splendid new winery was built at the top of the hill. Pinot Noir is about 85% of production.

The focus is on Sonoma, with appellation bottlings from Central Coast, Sonoma County, and Russian River Valley appellation bottlings, extending to an impressive series of single vineyard wines from top sites. More than half comes from estate vineyards, the rest from vineyards under long-term contracts that Williams-Selyem farms. More recently the range has been extended into Anderson Valley and Mendocino. There are typically six blended Pinot Noirs and 19 single vineyard wines, together with some Chardonnays and Zinfandels. Alcohol is reasonable because picking is usually at 23-24 Brix. "If you farm right, you can get ripe tannins at relatively low Brix." A focus on heritage clones may be a contributory factor to the restrained house style of Pinot Noir. "Williams Selyem is largely a Dijon clone-free zone," says Bob Cabral.

Winemaking is straightforward, with 20-25% use of whole clusters, five day cold soak, and addition of Williams Selyem's own strain of yeast to start fermentation. "It's very cookbook winemaking" says Bob Cabral. "Whether I'm making a $30 or $100 Pinot, the only real variable will be the proportion of new oak, from 40 for Russian River to up to 80% for single vineyards." In fact, wines are still made basically the way Burt made them, the most unusual feature being the use of dairy tanks to start off the cold soak. "This gives a very fine ratio of juice to skins, and foot treading gives light extraction," Jeff explains. There is no fining or filtration.

One legacy of Williams' winemaking is the use of low sulfur levels (10-15 ppm), as Burt was allergic to sulfur.

"The commonality is that the wines are all made in the same way," Jeff says, but Russian River AVA Pinot Noir is the most straightforward, Allen Vineyard is a little more viscous with a sense of underlying minerality, Westside Road neighbors is richer and deeper. Aromatics move from raspberries to strawberries to red cherries along the series. Olivet Lane and the Estate Vineyard are sterner and more structured. More than 90% of the single vineyard production sells to the mailing list, so the wines can be hard to find.

Carneros

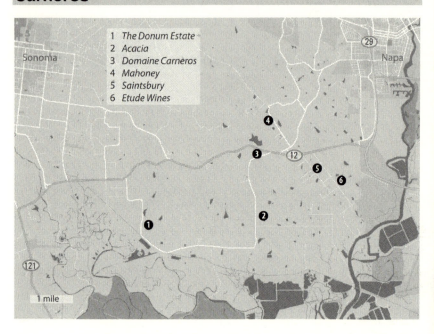

1 The Donum Estate
2 Acacia
3 Domaine Carneros
4 Mahoney
5 Saintsbury
6 Etude Wines

The Donum Estate

24500 Ramal Rd, Sonoma, CA 95476
(1) 707 732 2202
Anne Moller Racke
maggie@thedonumestate.com
www.thedonumestate.com
Carneros
Carneros, Pinot Noir
$80
130 acres; 60,000 bottles
[map p. 146]

The Donum Estate was created in 2001. Previously it had been part of the Buena Vista Carneros vineyards, but when the Moller Racke family sold Buena Vista to Allied Domecq, 200 acres of the 1,000 acres of vineyards were split off to form the Donum Estate. These include 45 acres in the old Tula Vista Ranch in Carneros (where Donum is located), 20 acres of the well known Ferguson Block a mile way, and another 11 ha of the Nugent Ranch in Russian River; some of the Carneros vineyards were sold in 2011. Almost all plantings are Pinot Noir; there is just a little Chardonnay.

The vineyards were mostly planted in the late 1980s and 1990s at a time when there was more emphasis on rootstocks than clones. Plantings include a clone obtained from Roederer Estate in Anderson Valley, but it seems to be distinct from the clones that Roederer uses for sparkling wine production, as it has small berries with thick skins that produce dark wines. This is now known as the Donum clone. Some vineyards were grafted over to Dijon clones in 2001 and 2004. The headquarters for vineyard operations are on the Carneros ranch, but wine is made at a custom crush facility in Russian River.

There are two labels: Donum Estate itself and also Robert Stemmler, which mostly represent different vineyard blocks, but with some barrel selection. When Donum started, they made only one wine, but then decided to move to single vineyard designations. Presently there are 6 different Pinots under the Donum label and 3 under Stemmler. "I have been thinking about stylistic aims because we get blame because the wines are so intense. They are vineyard-driven more than by winemaking techniques. I do like wines with concentration, but I do not want to lose delicacy," says Anne Moller Racke.

The estate was sold to a partnership of Danish investors in 2011, but management stays the same.

148 — Treasury Wine Estates

Etude Wines **

1250 Cuttings Wharf Road, Napa, CA 94559

(1) 707 257 5300

Gregory Sweval

EtudeInfo@EtudeWines.com

www.etudewines.com

Carneros

Carneros Estate Pinot Noir

$25

281 acres; 420,000 bottles [map p. 146]

The winery in which Etude is now located was originally built by Remy Martin, who planted vineyards to provide a source of inexpensive grapes for brandy. "By the mid nineties the brandy was too good—it cut into sales of brandy from France—so they shut it down." says manager Gregory Sweval at Etude. Etude wines was founded by Tony Soter in 1982 and sold to Beringer in 2001; then in 2002 Beringer brought the facility from Remy Martin to be the new headquarters for Etude. It became part of Treasury when they took over Beringer. It's a very large facility, a bit under used relative to present production. The old distillery is now an empty warehouse and will be converted to a barrel room. The ranch around the winery is still planted with low quality varieties (they are sold off), and in fact all the grapes for Etude's production come from Grace Benoist Ranch, 20 miles to the north in the northwest corner of Carneros just south of Sonoma.

Pinot Noir is 90% of production. The ranch varies from flat at the south to rolling hills at the north, and the Estate Pinot, which is about a third of all production, is a blend from parcels across the ranch. In addition there are three cuvées from individual blocks within the ranch. Until 2011 Etude made Pinot Noir only from Carneros. In 2012 it expanded the program to include other locations, which now include Sonoma Coast, Santa Rita Hills to the south, and Willamette in Oregon. All the grapes are trucked to the winery in refrigerated trucks, except for a cuvée from New Zealand which is made in situ. The wines from Carneros are the most fragrant and immediately attractive, Sonoma Coast shows cool climate restraint, Santa Rita Hills is more powerfully structured, and Central Otago is tougher. A Pinot tasting at Etude is an education in the effects of location, as all the wines are made by the same winemaker

Within the Carneros cuvées, the elegant house style is smooth and silky, with increasing tendency to move from tea-like to chocolate tannin impressions on the finish as you go from the estate blend to the individual blocks. The wines are reminiscent of Carneros's original objectives, to make Pinot Noir in a lighter, elegant style. In addition there are Chardonnays from Carneros and Cabernet Sauvignons from Napa: the Cabernets include a blend from all sites, and separate cuvées from St. Helena, Rutherford, and Oakville. The house style favors tightly structured wines that need time to develop.

Saintsbury

1500 Los Carneros Ave, Napa, CA 94559
(1) 707 252 0592
David Graves
info@saintsbury.com
www.saintsbury.com
Carneros
Carneros, Lees Vineyard, Pinot Noir
$35
360,000 bottles
[map p. 146]

Saintsbury was established in 1981 when Dick Ward and David Graves, who met at oenology classes at UC Davis, decided on Carneros for their vineyard because of its history with Pinot Noir. They have always purchased most of their fruit, although they grow a higher percentage of Pinot Noir than other varieties. Their own vineyards are the home ranch, the RMS vineyard just down the road, and the Brown Ranch, which comprise 12 ha of the total 21 ha from which they source grapes. They have control of the viticulture at vineyards where they buy grapes. Dick Ward died in 2017

In 1983 it became apparent that individual vineyards varied differently in each vintage so they split production into regular production and the "Garnet" value bottlings intended for early drinking. The distinction was based on selection. However, the Garnet label was sold to Silverado Cellars in 2011. I

n 1990 they started to make a Reserve Pinot Noir, then they moved to single vine-yard bottlings in 2004. Grapes are destemmed, there is cold soak for a few days, followed by a mix of natural and inoculated fermentation. Blends use 15-25% new oak; the single vineyard wines use 30-40% new oak. All of the appellation blends are under 14% alcohol; the single vineyards are under 14.5%. Single vineyard wines are about 10% of total production. The wines age well, reaching a turning point with sous bois showing within a decade, but then they continue to develop beautifully and slowly for another decade.

Santa Cruz

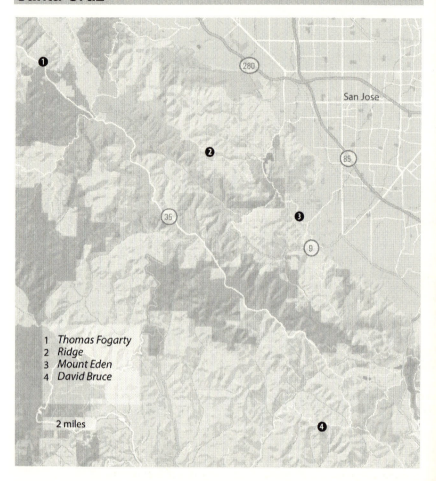

1 *Thomas Fogarty*
2 *Ridge*
3 *Mount Eden*
4 *David Bruce*

2 miles

Thomas Fogarty Winery   *

5937 Alpine Road, Portola Valley, CA 94028
(1) 650 851 6777
Nathan Kandler
info@fogartywinery.com
www.fogartywinery.com
Santa Cruz Mountains
Santa Cruz Mountains, Rapley Trail, Pinot Noir
144,000 bottles
[map p. 150]

The eponymous Thomas Fogarty (a surgeon at Stanford) owned this land before he decided to make wine. The vineyards were planted in 1978 and Michael Martella came as the winemaker in 1981. The location has spectacular views all the way out to San Francisco Bay, at a sufficient elevation that you see the blimp cruising along below. Except for one vineyard that is being replanted, all are still the original plantings. The vines came from the David Bruce vineyard or the Martini selection, and have since been supplemented with some Dijon and Swan clones. Originally the best selections went into a Reserve bottling, but Fogarty moved to single vineyard bottling in 2002. Around the winery all the vineyards are planted to Pinot Noir or Chardonnay; there are some Bordeaux varieties at another vineyard 20 minutes farther south. The major Pinot Noir vineyards are Windy Hill (right beside the winery) which is presently being replanted, and Rapley Trail. The 2 ha of the Rapley Trail vineyard are the only areas with clay in the soil (heavier at the top, thinner below); the rest is loam and sand. The Rapley Trail vineyard has now been subdivided into blocks, with the inventive names of M for the middle and B for the bottom; it is picked from bottom to top over a one month period.

Mount Eden Vineyards **

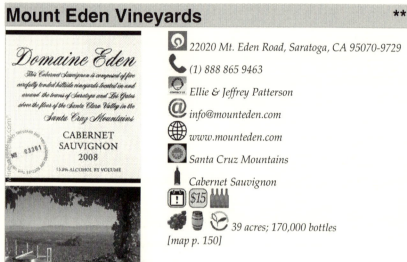

22020 Mt. Eden Road, Saratoga, CA 95070-9729

(1) 888 865 9463

Ellie & Jeffrey Patterson

info@mounteden.com

www.mounteden.com

Santa Cruz Mountains

Cabernet Sauvignon

$15

39 acres; 170,000 bottles

[map p. 150]

Driving up a precipitous dirt track on the edge of the Santa Cruz Mountains to the Mount Eden Winery with a solid sheet of water descending from the sky, I began to wonder whether current owner and winemaker Jeffrey Patterson had been euphemistic when he warned me the track was 2.2 miles long. But the drive was worth it. The Mount Eden Winery was originally the Martin Ray winery, created in the 1940s after Martin Ray had bought and then later sold the nearby Paul Masson winery. After Martin Ray left in 1970, this became the Mount Eden winery in 1972. There were several rapid changes in winemaker, until Jeffrey Patterson started making the wine in 1981.

The winery is perched at a height of about 2,100 feet, overlooking Santa Clara Valley; on a clear day you can see to the Pacific, 14 miles away. Mount Eden produces Cabernet Sauvignon, Pinot Noir, and Chardonnay, a clear indication that this is cool climate for Cabernet Sauvignon. The Estate Cabernet Sauvignon is a Bordeaux-like blend, usually with about 75% Cabernet Sauvignon. Until 2000, when the vines had to be replanted because they had finally stopped producing, there was also a bottling of an Old Vines Cabernet Sauvignon, a 100% selection of a plot of Cabernet planted on its own roots by Martin Ray in the 1950s. Only estate grapes are used except for the Edna Valley Chardonnay.

Ridge Vineyards ***

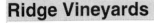

MONTE BELLO VINEYARD 74% CABERNET SAUVIGNON,
20% MERLOT, 4% PETIT VERDOT, 2% CABERNET FRANC
SANTA CRUZ MOUNTAINS 13.2% ALCOHOL BY VOLUME
GROWN, PRODUCED & BOTTLED BY RIDGE VINEYARDS
17100 MONTE BELLO ROAD, P.O. BOX 1810, CUPERTINO, CA 95015

 17100 Monte Bello Road, Cupertino, CA 95014

 (1) 408 867 3233

 Paul Draper

 wine@ridgewine.com

 www.ridgewine.com

 Santa Cruz Mountains

 Estate Cabernet Sauvignon

 439 acres; 600,000 bottles

[map p. 150]

The first vineyards and original Monte Bello Winery in the Santa Cruz mountains date from 1885. Ridge Vineyards was established in 1959 by a group of scientists from the Stanford Research Institute, who made the wine. Paul Draper came to Ridge in 1969. He tasted the 1962 and 1964 (both monovarietal Cabernets) and was impressed: "It was the first time I tasted California wine outside of the old Inglenook and Beaulieu wines with the complexity of Bordeaux. Those two wines were the reason why I joined Ridge." He became the managing partner and winemaker. The company was sold to a Japanese pharmaceutical company in 1987, but this does not seem to have made any difference. From the estate, extended along the ridge since the original purchase, come the famous Monte Bello Cabernet Sauvignon and Chardonnay. (Ridge is also famous for its single vineyard series of Zinfandels, which come from a wide range of locations, extending from Lytton Springs, Geyserville, and other vineyards in Sonoma, to a ranch in Paso Robles: see profile of Ridge Lytton Springs). Grapes come from both estate and purchased sources. Paul retired officially in 2016, but remains actively involved.

At the Monte Bello estate, 24 parcels are usually used for producing the Monte Bello Cabernet, and another 21 for the Estate Cabernet. There are about 42 ha of vineyards for the black varieties altogether. The Estate Cabernet is essentially a second wine, although each parcel—or sometimes half parcel—is assessed separately. Decisions are made on most parcels before an initial assemblage, but some are left to be reassessed later, and one or two parcels change destination each year. The approach is distinctly Bordelais, with a perspective of viewing lots as more important than varieties. Paul shows some disdain for the modern style of full-blown Cabernets, and Monte Bello remains a classic: it's a long-lived wine, and Paul thinks it begin to show its characteristics around 9-12 years, developing until 20 or 30 years. The Monte Bello Chardonnay, made only in small quantities, is one of California's most European-style white wines. "Monte Bello is one of the few places in California that has limestone and we feel that is important for the making of Chardonnay," says winemaker Paul Olney at Ridge Lytton Springs.

Monte Bello is a blend, and perhaps not surprisingly considering Paul's traditional imperatives, closer to Bordeaux in its varietal composition than to a Napa Cabernet. The transition took a while, from the monovarietal of the early sixties, to a wine with over 90% Cabernet Sauvignon in the eighties, and then to a range over the past two decades from a minimum of 56% to a maximum of 85%. Merlot is always the second most important variety, with smaller amounts of Petit Verdot and Cabernet Franc. Monte Bello is a long-lived wine; Paul thinks it begin to show its characteristics around 9-12 years of age, and develops until it is 20 or 30 years old. As for really old vintages, the 1974 was only just past its peak at 35 years of age, and the 1964 was rather tertiary but still enjoyable at 45 years. I can't help but wonder how much the moderate style of the wines is a key factor in ensuring such longevity.

Mount Harlan: Calera Wine Company ***

- 11300 Cienega Road, Hollister, CA 95023
- (1) 831 637 9170
- Josh Jensen
- info@calerawine.com
- www.calerawine.com
- Mount Harlan
- Mount Harlan, Mills Vineyard, Pinot Noir
- $10
- 82 acres; 400,000 bottles

Calera is sui generis. There is no other vineyard within fifty miles, there probably isn't any other vineyard in California at such a high elevation, and certainly there is none with limestone soils. The six vineyards of Pinot Noir total 36 ha; there are another 7 ha of Chardonnay and Viognier. Estate fruit is used for the single vineyards and Mount Harlan cuvée; purchased fruit is the basis of the Central Coast bottling. The winery (much lower down the mountain than the vineyards themselves) was converted from an old rock-crushing facility. Before a recent makeover, it was famous as one of the ugliest wineries around. It now houses a multi-storey gravity-fed winemaking facility (with a tasting room at one end for fans who make the pilgrimage up the mountain). Winemaking follows conventional Burgundian principles; the single vineyard wines spend 16 months in oak, 30% of which is new for most vineyards in most vintages.

In the earliest vintages, from 1978-1981, the aim was to have 12.5% alcohol. Then Josh started picking a little later to get greater ripeness, and the wines went to 13.5%. In the past decade there's been some bracket creep, picking a little riper each year, but Josh says that since 2005 there's been a pull back to earlier picking. Usually each vineyard is harvested in several batches, typically producing more sugar (higher potential alcohol) in the later pickings. The assemblage can give more complexity than a single picking. "If you aspire to make great wines, you often have to take risks, you are living on a knife's edge between picking too early and picking too late," says Josh.

There are six vineyards. Selleck, Jensen, and Reed were planted in 1975; Mills, Ryan, and De Villiers were planted between 1984 and 2001. (Mills vineyard is on its own roots; the soil may be sandy enough to have some resistance to phylloxera, and the vineyards are isolated.) De Villiers, Mills, and Reed are on the lighter side with a red fruit spectrum, Ryan offering a half way house, and Jensen and Selleck show greater density and structure in a black fruit spectrum. The two vineyards that give the most different wines are Selleck and Reed, close together but on opposite sides of a stream with opposed aspects. Selleck faces south and makes Calera's most intense wine; Reed faces north and makes the lightest wine. Jensen and Selleck are the wines with most aging potential. I felt Josh had gone a long way towards proving his point about aging on limestone when I tasted the 1990 Jensen vineyard, whose savory notes and delicious tones of sous bois seemed quite Burgundian at more than twenty years of age. Perhaps it ages a little more quickly than Burgundy.

Calera is such an idiosyncratic operation that it's hard to imagine it under any management other than Josh Jensen, but it was sold to Duckhorn, a large producer with several brands from the North Coast, in 2017. Josh Jensen and the rest of the team remain.

Mini-Profiles of Important Estates

Napa

Accendo Cellars

Wheeler Farms, 588 Zinfandel Lane, St. Helena, CA 94574
(1) 707 963 1989
Bart & Daphne Araujo
visits@accendocellars.com
accendocellars.com

 16,000 bottles

After Bart and Daphne Araujo purchased the Eisele vineyard in 1991, they produced Cabernet Sauvignon (and other varieties) under the name of Araujo Estate. They sold the estate to François Pinault of Château Latour in 2013, and its name was later changed to Eisele Vineyard Estate (see profile). The Araujos started a new venture, which they called Accendo Cellars, based on sourcing grapes from top sources to supplement production from plots in St. Helena and Oak Knoll. They created a custom crush facility at Wheeler Farms in St. Helena, and the wine is made there. The same team is involved as at the old Araujo Estate, including the next Araujo generation, Jaime and Greg, and Michel Rolland as consultant. The focus is on the same varieties as at Araujo: production is split more or less equally between Cabernet Sauvignon and Sauvignon Blanc.. The objective remains to make wine in a Bordelais style.

Anderson's Conn Valley Vineyards

680 Rossi Road, St. Helena, CA 94574
(1) 707 963 8600
Todd Anderson
cvvinfo@connvalleyvineyards.com
connvalleyvineyards.com

 39 acres; 96,000 bottles
[map p. 49]

Gus Anderson was an orthodontist in Michigan before he moved to California. In 1981, he started a new career by purchasing land in Conn Valley, just south of Howell Mountain. He started by planting a vineyard and selling grapes, and then together with his son Todd established a winery. The first vintage was 1987. Gus handed over to Todd in 2001, although he then started a new project, Eagle Trace Winery, which he ran until 2015. The focus is on high-end Cabernet blends: Eloge usually has about 50% Cabernet Sauvignon, while Right Bank has a majority of Cabernet Franc. The flagship wine is the Estate Reserve, which is almost pure Cabernet Sauvignon. At one extreme there are also some micro-cuvées; at the other, in 2015 a second wine was introduced, just labeled Napa Valley Cabernet Sauvignon. There are also Pinot Noir, Chardonnay, and a white Bordeaux blend.

B cellars

703 Oakville Cross Road, Oakville, CA 94562
(1) 707 709 8787
info@bcellars.com
www.bcellars.com

 60,000 bottles
[map p. 50]

Jim Borsack and Duffy Keys were businessmen when they met in 2002. A year later they abandoned their former careers and started B cellars. Grapes come from a variety of sources in Napa—18 different vineyards at last count—and initially wines were made in custom crush facilities. Kirk Venge has been the winemaker from the start. The B cellars winery in Oakville was opened in 2014. Tastings take place in the so-called Hospitality House. In addition to 5 Beckstoffer cuvées (all Cabernet Sauvignon except for Dr. Crane Cabernet Franc), there are 5 100% Cabernet Sauvignons from different sites. There are also Proprietary Blends, including some unexpected combinations, and Sauvignon Blanc and Chardonnay. Most cuvées are produced in less than 200 cases.

Cain Vineyard & Winery

3800 Langtry Road, St. Helena, Napa Valley, CA
(1) 707 963 1616
Gillian Murphy
winery@cainfive.com
www.cainfive.com

 86 acres; 144,000 bottles
[map p. 49]

Carter Cellars

1170 Tubbs Lane, Calistoga, CA 94515
(1) 707 445 0311
0
info@cartercellars.com
www.cartercellars.com

[map p. 49]

Clos du Val Winery

5330 Silverado Trail, Napa, CA 94558
(1) 707 259 2200
cmilan@closduval.com
www.closduval.com

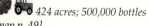 424 acres; 500,000 bottles
[map p. 49]

Continuum

1677 Sage Canyon Road, St. Helena, CA 94574
(1) 707 944 8100
Tim Mondavi
chelsea@continuumestate.com
www.continuumestate.com

 61 acres; 42,000 bottles
[map p. 49]

Cain is located well up Spring Mountain, to the west of St. Helena, with vineyards ranging from 1,400 to 2,100 ft. The Cains bough a 550 acre estate on the mountain in 1980, which had mostly been used as sheep pastures. They planted vineyards and constructed a winery; 1985 was the first vintage for Cain Five (named because it includes the five Bordeaux varieties, Cabernets Sauvignon and Franc, Merlot, Petit Verdot, and Malbec). Cabernet Sauvignon is more than half the plantings. Cain Five remains the flagship wine and is supplemented by Cain Cuvée (a blend of two vintages) and Cain Concept (from purchased grapes). A Sauvignon Blanc was made until 2002 from fruit purchased in Monterey.

Mark Carter founded Carter Cellars when he was running a hotel and restaurant in Eureka, in the far north of California. He commuted to Napa, where Carter Cellars started with the 1998 vintage, made with purchased grapes by winemaker Nils Venge in rented space. In 2006, Mark and Nils started another project, Envy Wines, with a 17 acres vineyard. The wines for Carter Cellars are now made at Envy Wines. Made in small quantities, they come from a roll call of famous vineyards. Almost all the cuvées are single vineyard Cabernet Sauvignons, including six from various Beckstoffer vineyards. The style is full force California.

Clos du Val classes as old-line winery in Napa, founded in 1972 by John Goelet and Bernard Portet (son of Château Lafite's technical director), whose aesthetic for winemaking was unsurprisingly French. The style was restrained and the tannins were evident. As Napa turned to riper and riper wines in the late 1990s, the style went out of fashion. This led to a change in approach in the early 2000s, followed more recently by restricting production to estate vineyards, and cutting back the total. From the original 125 acres in Stag's Leap, the flagship Cabernet Sauvignon is smooth and chocolaty. Other wines come from 120 acres in Yountville and 180 acres in Carneros.

Michael Mondavi was the winemaker at Robert Mondavi when the winery was sold to Constellation in 2004. He founded Continuum together with other family members shortly after the sale. Unlike Mondavi, which produced wines at all levels, Continuum focuses on the high end. Initially grapes were purchased from the To-Kalon vineyard close to Mondavi, then vineyards were purchased on Pritchard Hill to the east of the valley. By 2012, all grapes came from the estate vineyards. The winery was completed in time for the 2013 harvest. Continuum resembles a left bank Bordeaux blend, with about three quarters Cabernet Sauvignon. The sec-

Dalla Valle Vineyards

7776 Silverado Trail, Oakville, CA 94562
(1) 707 944 2676
Andy Erickson
info@dallavallevineyards.com
www.dallavallevineyards.com

 22 acres; 36,000 bottles
[map p. 50]

ond wine, Novicium, is about half Merlot, with the rest Cabernet Franc and Sauvignon. The style is richer than it was at Mondavi.

Naoko (originally from a Sake-producing family in Japan) and Gustav Dalla Valle (from a winemaking family in Italy) bought a property on a terrace 400 ft above the Silverado Trail in 1982. It came with a 3 acre vineyard, they purchased more land from neighboring properties, built a winery, and hired Heidi Barret as winemaker for the first vintage in 1986. Gustav died in 1995 and Naoko continued. The specialty is Cabernet Franc—"all our wines are blended with Cabernet Franc," says Naoko. The flagship wine, Maya (only 500 cases) is an equal blend of Cabernet Franc and Cabernet Sauvignon. The varietal Cabernet Sauvignon has a little Cabernet Franc; MDV is a cuvée from the best block of Cabernet Sauvignon. The latest cuvée is effectively a second wine, Collina, coming from younger vines and intended to be more approachable.

Flora Springs Winery

1978 W. Zinfandel Lane, St. Helena, CA 94574
(1) 707 963 5711
info@florasprings.com
www.florasprings.com

 498 acres; 240,000 bottles
[map p. 50]

It is hard to miss the Flora Springs tasting room as you drive up route 29 into St. Helena and see a striking building with an undulating roof. (They call it The Room.) The winery is up the hill at the end of Zinfandel Lane, and was where the venture started when Jerry and Flora Komes bought an old winery property in 1978 as a place to retire. Now in the third generation, Flora Springs has become one of the largest properties in Napa still in family hands. The wide range of wines extends from the standard Napa Valley varietals, to the flagship Trilogy, a blend of Cabernet Sauvignon with about 10% each of Malbec and Petit Verdot. There are also wines produced in smaller quantities and available only from the wine club or at the tasting room.

Freemark Abbey

3022 St. Helena Highway North, St. Helena, CA 94574
(1) 800 963 9698
Ted Edwards
wineinfo@freemarkabbey.com
www.freemarkabbey.com

  0 acres; 720,000 bottles
[map p. 50]

This venerable property dates from 1881. It took its present name in 1939 after a change of ownership. The modern era started when a group bought it in 1967 and focused on Cabernet Sauvignon. It was sold to an investor group in 2001, and then became part of Jackson Family Estates in 2006. The historic stone building was handsomely restored in 2016, and is open for a range of tours and tastings. Ted Edwards has been the winemaker since 1986. Freemark Abbey does not own vineyards, but sources fruit from growers, often on long term contracts. It is best known for its flagship Cabernet from the 22 acre Bosché vineyard on the Rutherford Bench (made since 1970). It usually has up to 18% Merlot, and production is less than 4,000 cases. I find this to offer one of the more European styles in Napa. The Chardonnay is known for its restrained style, emphasizing freshness by no malolactic fermentation, and limiting oak. Unusually for Napa, the winery also has a restaurant, open for lunch.

Frog's Leap Winery

8815 Conn Creek Rd, Rutherford, CA 94573
(1) 707 963 4704
John Williams
ribbit@frogsleap.com
www.frogsleap.com

 580 acres; 60,000 bottles

John Williams founded Frog's Leap together with Larry Turley in 1981 after making wine at Stag's Leap. The first releases were made from purchased grapes. Larry left to form Turley Wine Cellars, and John acquired the winery site in 1994: it was originally the site of the Adamson Winery in 1884, and the large red barn was refurbished to become Frog's Leap Winery. The home vineyard of 40 acres surrounds the winery, which also owns 88 acres in Rutherford as well as farming another 100 acres. The vineyards are dry farmed. The name is followed by a slightly zany approach, so tours can be slightly different here. Unusually for Napa, the focus was originally on Sauvignon Blanc and Zinfandel: Cabernet Sauvignon and other varieties followed as the estate vineyards came on line, but Sauvignon Blanc is still the flagship wine.

Gallica

3125 N St. Helena Highway, St. Helena, CA 94574
(1) 707 963 1096
Rosemary Cakebread
info@gallicawine.com
www.gallicawine.com

2 acres; 12,000 bottles [map p. 50]

Rosemary Cakebread started making wine at Inglenook, after graduating from UC Davis in oenology. She was the winemaker for Spottswoode from 1997 to 2005. (She worked briefly at Cakebread Cellars and is married to Bruce Cakebread.) She started Gallica Cellars in 2007, and makes wine from a mix of estate and purchased grapes from various sources. The flagship wine is Cabernet Sauvignon from Oakville, but she also produces wines from Rhône varieties, including Grenache from Sonoma and from Amador, and Syrah from Santa Lucia Highlands.

The Hess Collection

4411 Redwood Road, Napa, CA 94558
(1) 707 255 1144
info@hesscollection.com
hesscollection.com

 7,200,000 bottles [map p. 49]

The Hess Collection refers both to wine production and to the contemporary art collection at the museum next to the winery. Donald Hess, who comes from a family of beer brewers in Switzerland, created his vineyard about 2000 feet up Mount Veeder in 1978. The winery used to be one of the facilities used by the Christian Brothers. Hess is a very large producer, with several other wineries, and The Hess Collection represents about 10% of all production, concentrating on estate wines from Mount Veeder. The wines are well made, in a soft, crowd-pleasing style. Hess Select wines are made at a winery in American Canyon in southern Napa County.

Hourglass Wine Company

701 Lommel Road, Calistoga, CA 94515
(1) 707 968 9332
Jeff Smith
marybeth@hourglasswine.com
www.hourglasswine.com

Ned Smith bought a 6 acre parcel on Lodi Lane in 1976. It's called the Hourglass Vineyard because it's at the most constricted point of Napa Valley. Originally Ned and his son Jeff planted Zinfandel, but when it became necessary to replant in the 1990s, it was replaced by Cabernet Sauvignon. The Smiths bought the Blueline Vineyard, south of Calistoga, in 2006, and replanted it with Cabernet Sauvignon, Cabernet Franc, and Merlot. Bob Foley was the winemaker. The Hourglass Estate Cabernet Sauvignon

24 acres
[map p. 50]

Hundred Acre Vineyard

1345 Railroad Avenue, St. Helena, CA 94564
(1) 707 967 9398
Jayson Woodbridge
jayson@hundredacre.ca
www.hundredacre.com

 29 acres

The Kapcsandy Family Winery

1001 State Lane, Yountville, CA 94599
(1) 707 948 3100
Lou Kapcsándy
info@kapcsandywines.com
www.kapcsandywines.com

 $150

14 acres; 36,000 bottles
[map p. 50]

Kenzo Estate

3200 Monticello Road, Napa, CA 94558
(1) 707 254 7572
Tamamo Dughman
info@kenzoestate.com
www.kenzoestate.com

 $50
 150 acres; 200,000 bottles
[map p. 49]

is 100% varietal, from the Hourglass vineyard. From the Blueline Estate there are varietal Cabernet Sauvignon, Cabernet Franc, Merlot, and Malbec cuvées. There's also a Cabernet and Petit Verdot blend, the HGIII blend that includes some Italian varieties, and a Sauvignon Blanc (the only white wine).

Investment banker Jayson Woodbridge founded Hundred Acre in 2000 with the purchase of the 10 acre Kayli Morgan vineyard on the Silverado Trail between St. Helena and Calistoga. He subsequently purchased the 15 acre Ark vineyard on Howell Mountain, followed by the Few and Far Between parcel just above the Eisele vineyard. Each produces a 100% Cabernet Sauvignon in full-force style—needless to say, in 100% new oak—often with alcohol above 15%. The winery was constructed under the Ark vineyard in 2005. Philippe Melka made the initial vintages in 2000 and 2001, after which Jayson took over. Under the general rubric of One True Vine, Jayson also owns several other producers, making wines in more popular styles in California and Italy.

Lou Kapcsándy and his family purchased the State Lane Vineyard in Yountville, which had previously been the source for Beringer's Private Reserve Cabernet Sauvignon, in 2000, and replanted the vineyard in 2002. The winery was built in 2005. A self-confessed Francophile, his wines are intended to follow Bordeaux. "We dislike high-alcohol wines," he says, "Most of the wines we make have less than 14% alcohol." Nonetheless, the style tends to be powerful. Denis Malbec from Château Latour was the winemaker until he died in an accident in 2016. The flagship wine is the so-called Grand Vin, the State Lane Cabernet Sauvignon (90-99% Cabernet). The Estate Cuvée is a more typical Bordeaux blend, with about two thirds Cabernet Sauvignon. Roberta's Reserve is a 100% Merlot. Rhapszodia is a right-bank blend, two third Cabernet Franc to one third Merlot.

Kenzo Tsujimoto is Chairman of Japan's Capcom Group, a gaming company that produces the Street Fighter and Resident Evil video games. In 1990, he purchased 4,000 acres of an old equestrian ranch on Mount George. He had not originally intended to make wine, but in 2002 he brought in an all-star team and planted a vineyard, with David Abreu as the vineyard manager and Heidi Barrett as the consulting winemaker. The tasting room offers pairings of the wines with food created by Thomas Keller of the French Laundry. There are four wines: Rindo (the nearest thing to an entry-level wine) and Murasaki are Cabernet-based blends, Ai is a varietal Cabernet Sauvignon, and Asatsuyu is a Sauvignon Blanc. The winery was followed by a Japanese restaurant in downtown Napa, also called Kenzo.

La Jota Vineyard

1102 Las Posadas Road, Angwin, CA 94508
3299 Bennett Lane, Calistoga CA 94515 (tasting room)
(1) 877 222 0292
Chris Carpenter
info@lajotavineyardco.com
www.lajotavineyardco.com

📅 $65 🍷

🍇 🚜 27 acres; 42,000 bottles
[map p. 49]

La Jota is a boutique winery producing wines from two vineyards: the La Jota vineyard that surrounds the winery, which was built in 1898; and the W. S. Keyes vineyard a mile away, both on Howell Mountain between 1,700 and 1,900 ft elevation. The modern incarnation of La Jota dates from 1982; the Smiths who founded it sold to Markham Vineyards in 2001, who in turn sold it to Jackson Family Estates in 2003. La Jota produces varietal Cabernet Sauvignon and Cabernet Franc; the varietal Merlot comes from the W. S. Keyes vineyard. The wines are rich but not overpowering: Cabernet Sauvignon is the most forceful, Cabernet Franc is smoother with a touch of tobacco, Merlot has the most aromatic lift and ends in bitter chocolate. They can be tasted at another Jackson property, Spire Collection near Calistoga.

Lail Vineyards

320 Stone Ridge Road, Angwin, CA 94508
(1) 707 968 9900
Chantal Leruitte
erin@lailvineyards.com
www.lailvineyards.com

📅 🍷

🍇 🛢 🚜 35,000 bottles
[map p. 49]

Robin Lail has a long history in Napa Valley. The daughter of John Daniels, who inherited Inglenook, she was a partner in the creation of Dominus. She founded her own estate in 1995, with two vineyards: Totem Vineyard in Yountville was part of the original Inglenook estate; and Mole Hill vineyard, where the winery is located, is about 1,600 ft up Howell Mountain. The flagship wine is the J. Daniel Cuvée, which is a Cabernet Sauvignon from various sources, as also is the Blueprint Cabernet (produced in larger amounts). Mole Hill Cabernet Sauvignon is a single vineyard release. There are two Sauvignon Blancs: Blueprint is aged in stainless steel and aims for crispness, whereas Georgia is aged entirely in new oak. As an alternative to going up the mountain to the winery, the wines can be tasted at Maisonry in Yountville.

Lokoya

3787 Spring Mountain Road, St. Helena CA 94574
(1) 707 948 1968
Bradley Wasserman
info@lokoya.com
www.lokoya.com

📅 $125 @

🍇 🍃 24,000 bottles
[map p. 49]

Lokoya is not so much a winery as a boutique brand name created in 1995 within Jackson Family Estates for a collection of varietal Cabernet Sauvignons from different mountain appellations: Mount Veeder, Howell Mountain, Diamond Mountain, and Spring Mountain. Chris Carpenter, who also makes the wines for another boutique operation within Jackson, La Jota Vineyard, is the winemaker. The style is similar: dense and rich, full of flavor but not overpowering, although with a marked tannic presence. The winery on Spring Mountain Road is a historic building, purchased by Jackson in 2013 and renovated in 2017, and the wines can be tasted there.

Outpost Wines

2075 Summit Lake Drive, Angwin, CA 94508
(1) 707 965 1718
info@outpostwines.com

Outpost is high on Howell Mountain, more or less at the top of Summit Lake Drive, at 2,100 ft elevation. It was established in 1998 by Frank and Kathy Dotzler. It is unusual for Napa, because the flagship variety is Zinfandel (although this has become something of a specialty around Angwin). There is, of course, a varietal Cabernet Sauvignon, but also Petite Syrah and

www.outpostwines.com

 19 acres
[map p. 49]

Grenache. The style is to harvest as late as possible for maximum ripeness. The Dotzlers are also partners in Mending Wall Winery, founded in 2014 together with winemaker Thomas Brown and others.

Peju Province Winery

8466 St. Helena Highway, Rutherford, CA 94573
(1) 800 446 7358
axel@peju.com
www.peju.com

 449 acres; 600,000 bottles
[map p. 50]

Tony and Herta Peju purchased 30 acres of vineyards in Rutherford in 1983: today Peju is a much larger operation, with the next generation of Lisa and Ariana now involved. A faux Castle, the winery is one of the more interesting buildings in the area. Vineyards are in Rutherford, Pope Valley, and Calistoga, and there is a wide range of wines, including varietal Merlot, Cabernet Franc, Petit Verdot, Syrah, Zinfandel, Piccolo in reds, and Viognier, Riesling, Sauvignon Blanc in whites, as well as rosé and sparkling wine. The style is soft and crowd-pleasing, with an impression almost of sweetness. The tasting room is one of the few remaining that is always open. Peju bought the old Acacia winery in Carneros and turned into their second estate, Liana, in 2016.

Pine Ridge Winery

5901 Silverado Trail, Napa, CA 94558
(1) 707 253 7500
info@pineridgewinery.com
www.pineridgewinery.com

308 acres; 1,000,000 bottles
[map p. 49]

Pine Ridge was one of the early wineries in Stag's Leap, founded in 1978, focused on Cabernet Sauvignon from the area. In 2000, the founding family sold it to Crimson Wine Group, which is part of Leucadia National Corp. Today Pine Ridge also produces Cabernet Sauvignon cuvées from Rutherford, Oakville, and Howell Mountain, as well as Napa Valley bottling, and Chardonnay from Carneros. The style has moved from the restraint of the early years to more forward, soft, aromatic fruits. There is also an inexpensive blend of Chenin Blanc which comes from northern California (near Sacramento). There is a focus on oenotourism at the winery, which has one of the more popular tasting rooms in the area.

Plumpjack

620 Oakville Cross Road, Oakville, CA 94562
(1) 707 945 1220
John Conover
tastingroom@plumpjack.com
www.plumpjackwinery.com

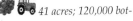 41 acres; 120,000 bottles
[map p. 50]

Plumpjack is located on the site of the old Villa Mount Eden Winery (a famous Cabernet producer from the 1970s until it was bought out in 1986 by Stimson Lane. In 1994, Stimson Lane sold the site and moved production elsewhere). Plumpjack was started by Gavin Newsom and Gordon Getty and other investors in 1995. Grapes come from the vineyards surrounding the winery. The flagship wine is the Estate Cabernet Sauvignon. The style is forward and aromatic. The Merlot, Syrah, and Chardonnay come from other sites. Plumpjack has expanded into a portfolio of wineries, purchasing a 54 acre estate on Howell Mountain in 2005 to form CADE winery, which was expanded by purchasing another 82 acres in 2016. In 2012 they bought the 36 acre Stelzner vineyard in Stags Leap, which became Winery Odette.

Robert Biale Vineyards

2040 Brown St, Napa, CA 94559
(1) 707 257 7555
tastingroom@biale.com
www.robertbialevineyards.com

   32 acres; 180,000 bottles
[map p. 49]

Robert Biale is unusual in Napa for focusing on Zinfandel: in fact, there is not even a single cuvée of Cabernet Sauvignon. The history of the Biale family was tied up with growing Zinfandel, and Robert started the winery with some partners in 1991. Today the winery produces 14 cuvées of Zinfandel, mostly from single vineyards. Estate grapes come from the small (8 acre) vineyard around the vineyard in Oak's Knoll and Aldo's vineyard, just south of the winery on the outskirts of Napa, which still has the original bush vines from 1937. Purchased grapes come from several vineyards in Sonoma. Biale also produces 5 cuvées of Petite Syrah.

Robert Craig Wine Cellars

625 Imperial Way, Napa, CA 94558 (tasting room)
2475 Summit Lake Drive, Angwin, CA 94508 (winery)
(1) 707 252 2250
info@robertcraigwine.com
www.robertcraigwine.com

    34 acres; 100,000 bottles
[map p. 49]

Robert Craig was always interested in mountain vineyards. He founded his own estate in 1992, and the first release was from Mount Veeder. The winery, well up Howell Mountain at an elevation of 2,300 ft, was completed in 2002. Robert retired in 2012, and his longtime partner Elton Slone now runs the winery. There are separate cuvées of Cabernet Sauvignon from Mount Veeder and Spring Mountain as well as Howell Mountain, as well as the Affinity cuvée, which comes from Mount George just south of Stag's Leap. They are generally about 90% Cabernet Sauvignon, with the rest coming from Cabernet Franc, Merlot, Malbec, or Petit Verdot. They are typical mountain wines, with dense black fruits and strong tannic support. There are also varietal Merlot and Zinfandel, and the latest cuvée is Côte de Craig, a Grenache-Syrah blend from Howell Mountain. All are single vineyard wines, with 80% of the grapes coming from the estate. The winery is not the most accessible, but there is a tasting room in downtown Napa.

St. Supéry Wines

8440 St. Helena Highway, Rutherford, CA 94573
(1) 707 963 4507
divinecab@stsupery.com
www.stsupery.com

 555 acres; 420,000 bottles
[map p. 50]

The Skalli family started making wine in Algeria, expanded into Corsica, and in 1982 bought the Dollarhide estate of over 1,500 acres, much of it used for cattle ranching, but including 500 acres of vineyards. Another 56 acres in Rutherford were bought in 1985, and the St. Supéry winery was constructed there in 1989. There are two lines of wines: Bordeaux varietals from the Rutherford estate; and a wider range from Dollarhide, including Chardonnay, Sauvignon Blanc, and Semillon. I have usually found the wines to be somewhat simple. The Wertheimer brothers of Chanel, who own Châteaux Rauzan-Ségla in Margaux and Canon in St. Emilion, bought St. Supéry in 2015. It will be interesting to see if the style changes.

165

Sterling Vineyards

1111 Dunaweal Lane, Calistoga, CA 94515
(1) 707 942 3344
svconcierge@svclub.com
www.sterlingvineyards.com

 1200 acres; 4,800,000 bottles
[map p. 49]

The most spectacular feature about Sterling is the approach, which makes it a major tourist site. The winery is located 300 ft above Calistoga, and access is by a small cable car. On one of my visits, the system stuck, and we were left swinging in the wind for half an hour. The winery was founded by Peter Newton in 1964, and released its first vintage in 1969: it was sold to Coca-Cola in 1977. (Peter Newton then started Newton Vineyard, which he later sold to LVMG.) Sterling was later sold to Seagram, became part of Diageo, and then was among the wineries sold to Treasury Wine Estates in 2015. In its heyday, Sterling was well regarded for its estate Cabernet and Chardonnay, which were among the wines that made the running in Napa in the early 1970s. Subsequent corporate takeovers turned it into a brand.

Tor Kenward Family Wines

Wheeler Farms, Zinfandel Lane, St. Helena, CA 94574
(1) 707 963 3100
Tor Kenward
info@torwines.com
www.torwines.com

0 acres; 40,000 bottles
[map p. 50]

Tor Kenward was an executive at Beringer before he retired and founded his own winery in 2001 to focus on small production runs of single vineyard Cabernet Sauvignon and Chardonnay. Grapes are purchased from top vineyards: production is less than 400 cases for each Cabernet cuvée and less than 100 cases for each Chardonnay. There are also cuvées of Syrah, Petite Syrah, and Grenache. Although there are no conventional winery visits at such, it's possible to make an appointment to visit at Wheeler Farms (a rather upmarket custom crush facility) or to taste the wines at Maisonry in Yountville.

Turley Wine Cellars

3358 St. Helena Highway, St. Helena, CA 94574
(1) 707 963 0940
Helen Turley
tasting@turleywinecellars.com
www.turleywinecellars.com

[map p. 50]

Larry Turley was a co-founder of Frog's Leap Winery (see mini-profile) but left to form an independent venture in 1993. The original winery is in St. Helena; a second winery was established later in Templeton in San Luis Obispo to the south). Wines can be tasted in Templeton but not in Napa. The focus is on Zinfandel, with 26 cuvées (most come from Central Coast, with a handful from farther north) and Petite Syrah (cuvées) out of a total of 47 wines coming from 50 different vineyards. Larry's sister is Helen Turley, another well known winemaker.

Vine Hill Ranch

2339 Picket Road, Calistoga, CA 94515
(1) 707 944 8130
Bruce Philipps
vhr@vinehillranch.com
vinehillranch.com

This is an old property, but its move to the modern style is more recent. Bruce Kelham purchased the ranch of more than 400 acres in 1959 on the slopes of the Mayacamas mountains when it was used for polyculture: farming hay (at the bottom), growing walnuts, and growing various grape varieties (but not Cabernet). Bruce's daughter Alexandra and her husband Bob Phillips took over in 1978 and started the move to current varieties when they were

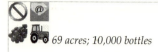 69 acres; 10,000 bottles

Whitehall Lane
1563 St. Helena Highway, St. Helena, CA 94574
(1) 707 963 9454
Katie Leonardini
greatwine@whitehalllane.com
www.whitehalllane.com

125 acres; 480,000 bottles
[map p. 50]

forced to replant by phylloxera in 1985. Their children run the property today. Originally all the grapes were sold, but since 2008 the Phillips have made a Cabernet Sauvignon as a selection from seven blocks. An original feature is that the label lists all seven blocks, and those used in any particular year are punched out on the label. The wine shows typical Oakville power and elegance.

The site has been growing grapes for a long time, but the existing winery was founded in 1979 by the Finklestein family, who sold it to the Leonardini family in 1993. In addition to the 25 acre estate vineyard around the winery, there are six vineyards in St. Helena, Rutherford, Yountville, and Oak Knoll, as well as one in Sonoma. There are Napa Valley varietal cuvées of Cabernet Sauvignon, Merlot, and Malbec, single vineyard wines from the Leonardini and Millennium MM vineyards in Rutherford, and the Oak Glen vineyard in Oak Knoll, a Zinfandel from Sonoma, and a single vineyard Pinot Noir from Carneros.

Sonoma

Arista Winery
7015 Westside Road, Healdsburg CA 95448
(1) 707 473 0606
Matt Courtney
daniel@aristawinery.com
www.aristawinery.com

37 acres; 60,000 bottles
[map p. 112]

"We are devoted to the potential of Pinot Noir from the Russian River Valley ," say the McWilliams, who founded Arista in 2002. Ben and Mark McWilliams took over from their parents in 2012. Matt Courtney came from assisting Helen Turley at Marcassin to be the winemaker. The estate vineyards are in the Middle Reach of Russian River, and grapes also come from six growers, mostly also in Russian River. There are Pinot Noir and Chardonnay appellation wines from Russian River, and also single vineyard wines from each of the growers. They purchased the Martinelli Road vineyard in 2012, with old vines Zinfandel as well as Pinot Noir and Chardonnay, so there may soon be some new cuvées in the estate wines.

Aubert Vineyards
333 Silverado Trail N, Calistoga, CA 94515
(1) 707 942 4333
Mark Aubert
wine@aubertwines.com
www.aubertwines.com

20 acres; 120,000 bottles
[map p. 49]

After working at cult wineries, Peter Michael and Colgin, Mark Aubert founded his own estate in 2000. Wines were made at Colgin and a custom crush facility before the winery was built in Calistoga in 2010; however, the focus is on Chardonnay and (to a slightly lesser extent) Pinot Noir from Sonoma and Carneros. There are some small estate vineyards in Sonoma, but most of the grapes are sourced from famous vineyards, including Ritchie (the first Chardonnay in 2000, from Sonoma Coast) and Hyde (the coolest site, in Carneros). The UV series comprises the wines from estate vineyards. The style is full-bodied and has been described as hedonistic.

Benziger Family Winery

1883 London Ranch Road, Glen Ellen, CA 95442
(1) 707 935 3000
greatwine@benziger.com
www.benziger.com

 1,600,000 bottles
[map p. 112]

The name is now misleading, as Benziger was sold to The Wine Group (the world's third largest wine company) in 2015. Benziger was certainly very large anyway for a family-owned estate, but the focus was on high-end wines, whereas much of the Wine Group's sales are boxed wines. Benziger was founded when Mike Benziger and his father Bruno purchased a ranch in 1980. Their first brand was Glen Ellen, which they sold to Heublein in 1993. They then created Benziger, and established a leadership in green viticulture, being an early convert to biodynamics. They also took a lead in oenotourism, with a variety of tours and tastings at the property. There is a large range of wines, around 30 at last count, including 6 cuvées of Pinot Noir. A separate winery, Imagery, makes small production runs. After the sale, Mike Benziger turned to farming cannabis.

DeLoach

1791 Olivet Road, Santa Rosa, CA 95401
(1) 707 755 3300
Brian Mahoney
customerservice@deloachvineyards.com
deloachvineyards.com

 17 acres; 1,800,000 bottles
[map p. 112]

Deloach was a pioneering winery in starting in Russian River in 1975, but it became bankrupt in 2003, and was purchased by Boisset from Burgundy. The winery had started with Cabernet and Zinfandel, but Boisset moved towards Pinot Noir and Chardonnay, now each about 40% of production. Estate grapes from the biodynamic vineyards are only a very small part of production, and provide a Chardonnay, a Pinot Noir, and two single vineyard Pinot Noirs.

DuMOL Winery

1400 American Way, Windsor, CA 95492
(1) 707 948 7144
Andy Smith
winery@dumol.com
www.dumol.com

 54 acres; 200,000 bottles
[map p. 112]

Michael Verlander and Kerry Murphy started DuMOL as a project to produce Pinot Noir and Chardonnay in Burgundian style from Russian River. the first vintage in 1996 produced 150 cases of each variety from the Dutton Ranch vineyard. In 2003 they purchased the first estate vineyard, increasing production from 8,500 to 12,000 cases. Wines were made at a custom crush facility in Santa Rosa until they outgrew the facility and constructed their own winery in an industrial park in Windsor. The location was not a problem because "we do not need a tasting room," Kerry Murphy said.

Hartford Family Winery

8075 Martinelli Road, Forestville CA 95436 (winery)
at 331 Healdsburg Avenue, Healdsburg, CA 95448 (tasting room)
(1) 707 887 1756
Hartford
hartford.winery@hartfordwines.com
www.hartfordwines.com

[$15]

101 acres; 175,000 bottles
[map p. 112] 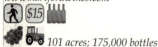 *Kendall-Jackson*

Don and Jenny Hartford (Jess Jackson's daughter) bought a property in 1991, and it came with a vineyard including some old Zinfandel. They founded the wine estate in 1994, and today produce a range of single-vineyard Pinot Noirs, Chardonnay, and old vines Zinfandel. Pinot Noir comes from Russian River Valley, Green Valley, Sonoma Coast, Carneros, and Anderson Valley. As the Hartfords describe their style: "Our number one goal at Hartford Family Winery is to make intensely concentrated wines." The wines can be tasted at the winery and also at a tasting room in downtown Healdsburg.

Marcassin Vineyard

7331 Conde Lane, Windsor, CA 95492
(1) 707 942 5633
John Wetlaufer
marcassinvineyards.com

24 acres; 33,000 bottles
[map p. 112]

Marcassin is controversial, not just for the character of its wine, but for comments John Wetlaufer made after a tasting in 2011, unfavorably comparing top white and red Burgundies with Marcassin wines—the La Tâche 2006 "was literally undrinkable" —because the Burgundies were unripe, compared to the super-ripeness of Marcassin. Marcassin is the label for famed consultant Helen Turley's production of her own wines, together with her husband John Wetlaufer, from an estate on Sonoma coast, at an elevation of 1,400 ft, 3 miles from the Pacific. (Until 2010, grapes came from other sources, and the wines were made at a neighboring winery.) Although the Sonoma Coast has come into fashion for the ability to make cooler climate wines than elsewhere in Sonoma, the Marcassin wines are über-ripe, with powerful fruits and high alcohol, in the typical Turley style. There is a waiting list of several years to obtain an allocation.

Ravenswood Winery

18701 Gehricke Road, Sonoma, CA 95476
(1) 707 938 1960
David Miles
rwwine@ravenswoodwinery.com
www.ravenswoodwinery.com

[$25]

34 acres; 12,000,000 bottles
[map p. 112] *Constellation*

Joel Peterson's motto when he founded Ravenswood in 1976 was "no wimpy wines." Given that motto, it is not surprising that the variety of choice was Zinfandel. Ravenswood's reputation was established by a series of single-vineyard Zinfandels from old vines. However, Joel kept his day job at Sonoma Valley Hospital until 1992. As Ravenswood expanded, cash flow demands led to the creation of the Vintners Blend range of six varieties, entry-level wines described as "not too dry." Ravenswood was sold to Constellation in 2001, and production more than doubled. Joel stayed on until 2016, when he started another project to make wines on a small scale.

Silver Oak Cellars

915 Oakville Crossroad, Oakville, CA 94562 (Napa Winery)
7300 Hwy 128, Healdsburg CA 95458 (Alexander Valley winery),United States
(1) 800 273 8809/ (707) 942 7026
info@silveroak.com
www.silveroak.com

 400 acres; 1,200,000 bottles
[map p. 50]

Silver Oak started as a collaboration between entrepreneur Ray Duncan and winemaker Justin Meyer to produce Cabernet Sauvignon in an approachable style. The first estate vineyards were located in Alexander Valley and were the basis for the wine from the first vintage in 1972. The cellars in Napa Valley were built on the site of an old dairy farm, but the Napa vineyards did not come on line until 1979. The Alexander Valley cuvée is 100% Cabernet Sauvignon; the Napa Valley cuvée, which comes from a mix of estate and purchased grapes, is a Bordeaux blend based on Cabernet Sauvignon. The wines are aged in American oak, which explains their strong impression of vanillin and coconut; indeed, at one time the winery was known as Slather Oak in the trade. Justin Meyer sold back his share in the company to Ray Duncan in 2001. A second winery was built in Geyserville, and was replaced by a new winery close to Healdsburg in 2018. The company is run today by Ray's sons, David and Tim. They also own Twomey Cellars, producing Pinot Noir and Sauvignon Blanc, from wineries in Calistoga and Healdsburg. In 2017, Silver Oak purchased the Ovid winery and its 15 acres of vineyards on Pritchard Hill.

Carneros

Acacia Winery

2750 Las Amigas Road, Napa, CA 94559
(1) 707 226 9991
acacia.info@acaciawinery.com
www.acaciavineyard.com

[map p. 146]

Acacia was one of the pioneers in Carneros, founded in 1979 with the intention of making Pinot Noir and Chardonnay in Burgundian style. In 1986 it was sold to Chalone, and in 2005 Chalone became part of Diageo. When Treasury Wine Estates purchased Diageo's wine interests in 2015, they acquired the Acacia brand name, but not the winery and surrounding 100 acre estate, which were sold in 2016 to Peju Province (see mini-profile), and were reopened as Liana Estates. The Acacia wines have always had a light, restrained style, and the original range has been extended into A by Acacia, entry-level wines from Central Coast.

Domaine Carneros

1240 Duhig Road, Napa, CA 94559
(1) 707 257 0101
Eileen Crane
tours@domainecarneros.com
www.domainecarneros.com

 840,000 bottles
[map p. 146]

This is Champagne Taittinger's venture into the New World, founded in 1987. The building is an imposing chateau in the French style. The first release was 3,000 cases of nonvintage Brut; in 1991 the wines started to be vintage-dated (except for the rosé). There is the same range of wines as in Champagne: Brut, Blanc de Blancs, and Blanc de Noirs. There is a focus on Pinot Noir, and the sparkling wines are extended by a range of 5 still varietal Pinot Noirs, including 4 single vineyard wines.

Mahoney Vineyards
1285 Dealy Lane, Napa, CA 94559
(1) 707 253 9464
Francis Mahoney
wineinfo@mahoneyvineyards.com
carneroswinecompany.com

160 acres
[map p. 146]

Francis Mahoney is a grape grower *par excellence*, and was a pioneer in establishing Pinot Noir in Carneros in the late 1970s when he owned Carneros Creek Winery, which he sold in 2002. Retirement was brief. Carneros Creek subsequently hit some difficulties, and he found himself looking after the vineyards again. "I've been investigating clones for 40 years," he says, and his mile of vineyards is organized into small blocks, with 149 acres planted with Pinot Noir. Francis remains principally a grower, but has been making wine from a small part of the crop since 2004. He also owns the Fleur de California brand. Tasting with him is an exercise in spotting subtle differences that come from different clones.

Santa Cruz

David Bruce Winery
21439 Bear Creek Road, Los Gatos, CA 95030
(1) 408 354 4214
info@davidbrucewinery.com
www.davidbrucewinery.com

   720,000 bottles
[map p. 150]

David Bruce was a dermatologist when he established this winery in 1964, close to the famous Martin Ray Vineyard, with the idea that the elevation of 2,200 ft would allow cool-climate production of Pinot Noir and Chardonnay. David Bruce eventually gave up medicine and became known as an innovator in wine. The winery became known for its focus on Pinot Noir, but in addition to the ten Pinot Noir cuvées, with grapes are sourced from all over California, there are also many other varietal wines. The diversity of sources means that the wines have somewhat lost their focus.

Index of Estates by Rating

3 star
Bryant Family Vineyard
Calera Wine Company
Harlan Estate
Opus One
Ridge Vineyards
Screaming Eagle Winery

2 star
Abreu Vineyards
Amapola Creek
Arrowood Winery
Beringer Vineyards
Chappellet Vineyard
Colgin Cellars
Corison Winery
Diamond Creek Vineyards
Dominus Estate
Dunn Vineyards
Eisele Vineyard Estate
Etude Wines
Joseph Phelps Vineyards
Kongsgaard Wine
Kosta Browne Winery
Merry Edwards Wines
Chateau Montelena
Morlet Family Vineyards
Mount Eden Vineyards
Newton Vineyard
Pahlmeyer Winery
Patz & Hall Wine Co.
Paul Hobbs Winery
Peter Michael
Pride Mountain Vineyards
Ridge Vineyards (Lytton Springs)
Robert Foley
Rodney Strong Vineyards
Sbragia Family Vineyards
Schrader Cellars
Shafer Vineyards
Williams Selyem

1 star
Alpha Omega Winery
Beaulieu Vineyards
Bell Wine Cellars
Cakebread Cellars
Carlisle Winery & Vineyards
Caymus Vineyards
Chalk Hill Estate
Domaine Chandon Winery
Chase Family Cellars
Chateau St. Jean
Dehlinger Winery
The Donum Estate
Far Niente
Thomas Fogarty Winery
Gary Farrell Wines
Grgich Hills Estate
Groth Vineyards & Winery
HALL
Heitz Cellars
Inglenook
Jarvis Winery
Jordan Vineyard & Winery
Joseph Swan Vineyards
Kamen Wines
Kistler Vineyards
Larkmead Vineyards
Littorai Wines
Louis Martini Winery
Martinelli Winery & Vineyards
Matanzas Creek Winery
Mayacamas Vineyards
Nickel & Nickel
Philip Togni Vineyard
Ramey Wine Cellars
Robert Mondavi Winery
Rochioli Vineyards & Winery
Saintsbury
Robert Sinskey Vineyards
Spottswoode Estate Vineyard & Winery
Stag's Leap Wine Cellars
Staglin Family Vineyard
Stonestreet
Trefethen Vineyards
Turnbull Wine Cellars
Vérité
Viader Vineyards
Vineyard 29
Walter Hansel
ZD Wines

Index of Organic and Biodynamic Estates

Amapola Creek
Benziger Family Winery
Cain Vineyard & Winery
Domaine Carneros
Chappellet Vineyard
Corison Winery
DeLoach
Eisele Vineyard Estate
Far Niente
Frog's Leap Winery
Gallica
Grgich Hills Estate
Heitz Cellars
Kamen Wines
Kongsgaard Wine
Littorai Wines
Paul Hobbs Winery
Robert Craig Wine Cellars
Robert Sinskey Vineyards
Spottswoode Estate Vineyard & Winery
Staglin Family Vineyard
ZD Wines

Index of Estates by Varietal Specialty

Cabernet Sauvignon
Abreu Vineyards
Accendo Cellars
Alpha Omega Winery
Amapola Creek
Anderson's Conn Valley
Arrowood Winery
B Cellars
Bryant Family Vineyard
Beaulieu Vineyards
Bell Wine Cellars
Beaulieu Vineyards
Carter Cellars
Caymus Vineyards
Chappellet Vineyard
Chateau Montelena
Clos du Val
Colgin Cellars
Continuum
Corison Winery
Diamond Creek Vineyards
Dominus Estate
Dunn Vineyards
Eisele Vineyard
Far Niente
Freemark Abbey
Gallica
Grgich Hills Estate
Groth Vineyards & Winery
Harlan Estate
Heitz Cellars
Hourglass
Hundred Acre
Inglenook
Jordan Vineyard & Winery
Joseph Phelps Vineyards
Kamen Wines
Kapcasandy
Kenzo
Lail Vineyards
Larkmead Vineyards
Lokoya
Mayacamas Vineyards
Mount Eden Vineyards
Nickel & Nickel
Opus One
Pahlmeyer Winery
Pride Mountain Vineyards
Ridge Vineyards
Rodney Strong Vineyards
Robert Foley
Robert Mondavi Winery
Sbragia Family Vineyards
Schrader Cellars
Screaming Eagle Winery
Shafer Vineyards
Spottswoode Estate Vineyard
Stag's Leap Wine Cellars
Staglin Family Vineyard
Stonestreet
Philip Togni Vineyard
Tor Kenward
Trefethen Vineyards
Turnbull Wine Cellars
Bordeaux Blend
Cain Vineyard
Chateau St. Jean
Vérité
Pinot Noir
Arista
David Bruce
Calera Wine Company
Dehlinger Winery
DuMOL
Etude Wines
Mahoney Vineyards
Marcassin
Gary Farrell Wines
Joseph Swan Vineyards
Kosta Browne Winery
Littorai Wines
Marcassin
Merry Edwards Wines
Paul Hobbs Winery
Robert Sinskey Vineyards
Rochioli Vineyards & Winery
Saintsbury
The Donum Estate
Thomas Fogarty Winery
Williams Selyem
Zinfandel
Robert Biali

Carlisle Winery & Vineyards
Chase Family Cellars
Hartford Family
Louis Martini Winery
Martinelli Winery & Vineyards
Outpost Wines
Ravenswood
Ridge Vineyards (Lytton Springs)
Seghesio
Turley Wine Cellars
   Chardonnay
Aubert
Cakebread Cellars
Chalk Hill Estate
Chateau Montelena
Kistler Vineyards
Kongsgaard Wine
Merryvale
Patz & Hall Wine Co.
Peter Michael
Ramey Wine Cellars
   Sauvignon Blanc
Matanzas Creek Winery
Robert Mondavi Winery
Sparkling Wine
Domaine Carneros
Domaine Chandon Winery

Index of Estates by Appellation

Alexander Valley
Jordan Vineyard & Winery
Silver Oak Cellars
Stonestreet

Atlas Peak
Kongsgaard Wine
Pahlmeyer Winery

Calistoga
Carter Cellars
Eisele Vineyard Estate
Hourglass Wine Company
Larkmead Vineyards
Chateau Montelena
Schrader Cellars
Sterling Vineyards

Carneros
Acacia Winery
Domaine Carneros
The Donum Estate
Etude Wines
Mahoney Vineyards
Saintsbury

Diamond Mountain District
Diamond Creek Vineyards

Howell Mountain
Dunn Vineyards
Lail Vineyards
Newton Vineyard
Outpost Wines
Robert Foley
Viader Vineyards

Knights Valley
Peter Michael

Mount Harlan
Calera Wine Company

Mount Veeder
The Hess Collection
La Jota Vineyard
Mayacamas Vineyards
Robert Craig Wine Cellars

Napa Valley
Jarvis Winery

Kenzo Estate
Robert Biale Vineyards

Oak Knoll
Trefethen Vineyards

Oakville
B cellars
Dalla Valle Vineyards
Far Niente
Groth Vineyards & Winery
Harlan Estate
Nickel & Nickel
Opus One
Plumpjack
Robert Mondavi Winery
Screaming Eagle Winery
Turnbull Wine Cellars
Vine Hill Ranch

Russian River Valley
Carlisle Winery & Vineyards
DeLoach
DuMOL Winery
Gary Farrell Wines
Hartford Family Winery
Joseph Swan Vineyards
Kistler Vineyards
Kosta Browne Winery
Littorai Wines
Marcassin Vineyard
Martinelli Winery & Vineyards
Matanzas Creek Winery
Merry Edwards Wines
Ridge Vineyards (Lytton Springs)
Rochioli Vineyards & Winery
Rodney Strong Vineyards
Walter Hansel
Williams Selyem

Rutherford
Alpha Omega Winery
Beaulieu Vineyards
Cakebread Cellars
Caymus Vineyards
Frog's Leap Winery
Grgich Hills Estate
HALL
Hundred Acre Vineyard

Inglenook
Peju Province Winery
St. Supéry Wines
Staglin Family Vineyard
Whitehall Lane
ZD Wines

Santa Cruz Mountains
David Bruce Winery
Thomas Fogarty Winery
Mount Eden Vineyards
Ridge Vineyards

Sonoma County
Arista Winery
Aubert Vineyards

Sonoma Valley
Amapola Creek
Arrowood Winery
Benziger Family Winery
Chalk Hill Estate
Chateau St. Jean
Dehlinger Winery
Kamen Wines
Patz & Hall Wine Co.
Paul Hobbs Winery
Ramey Wine Cellars
Ravenswood Winery
Sbragia Family Vineyards
Vérité

Spring Mountain District
Cain Vineyard & Winery
Lokoya Winery
Pride Mountain Vineyards

St. Helena
Abreu Vineyards

Accendo Cellars
Anderson's Conn Valley Vineyards
Beringer Vineyards
Bryant Family Vineyard
Chappellet Vineyard
Chase Family Cellars
Colgin Cellars
Continuum
Corison Winery
Flora Springs Winery
Freemark Abbey
Gallica
Heitz Cellars
Joseph Phelps Vineyards
Louis Martini Winery
Morlet Family Vineyards
Philip Togni Vineyard
Spottswoode Estate Vineyard & Winery
Tor Kenward Family Wines
Turley Wine Cellars
Vineyard 29

Stags Leap District
Clos du Val Winery
Pine Ridge Winery
Shafer Vineyards
Robert Sinskey Vineyards
Stag's Leap Wine Cellars

Yountville
Bell Wine Cellars
Domaine Chandon Winery
Dominus Estate
The Kapcsandy Family Winery

Index of Estates by Name

Abreu Vineyards, 51
Acacia Winery, 169
Accendo Cellars, 157
Alpha Omega Winery, 53
Amapola Creek, 113
Anderson's Conn Valley Vineyards, 157
Arista Winery, 166
Arrowood Winery, 114
Aubert Vineyards, 166
B cellars, 157
Beaulieu Vineyards, 54
Bell Wine Cellars, 55
Benziger Family Winery, 167
Beringer Vineyards, 56
Bryant Family Vineyard, 58
Cain Vineyard & Winery, 158
Cakebread Cellars, 59
Calera Wine Company, 155
Carlisle Winery & Vineyards, 115
Domaine Carneros, 169
Carter Cellars, 158
Caymus Vineyards, 61
Chalk Hill Estate, 116
Domaine Chandon Winery, 62
Chappellet Vineyard, 63
Chase Family Cellars, 64
Chateau St. Jean, 117
Clos du Val Winery, 158
Colgin Cellars, 65
Continuum, 158
Corison Winery, 66
Dalla Valle Vineyards, 159
David Bruce Winery, 170
Dehlinger Winery, 118
DeLoach, 167
Diamond Creek Vineyards, 67
Dominus Estate, 69
The Donum Estate, 147
DuMOL Winery, 167
Dunn Vineyards, 71

Eisele Vineyard Estate, 72
Etude Wines, 148
Far Niente, 74
Flora Springs Winery, 159
Thomas Fogarty Winery, 151
Freemark Abbey, 159
Frog's Leap Winery, 160
Gallica, 160
Gary Farrell Wines, 119
Grgich Hills Estate, 75
Groth Vineyards & Winery, 76
HALL, 77
Harlan Estate, 78
Hartford Family Winery, 168
Heitz Cellars, 79
The Hess Collection, 160
Hourglass Wine Company, 160
Hundred Acre Vineyard, 161
Inglenook, 81
Jarvis Winery, 82
Jordan Vineyard & Winery, 120
Joseph Phelps Vineyards, 83
Joseph Swan Vineyards, 121
Kamen Wines, 122
The Kapcsandy Family Winery, 161
Kenzo Estate, 161
Kistler Vineyards, 123
Kongsgaard Wine, 84
Kosta Browne Winery, 124
La Jota Vineyard, 162
Lail Vineyards, 162
Larkmead Vineyards, 86
Littorai Wines, 125
Lokoya Winery, 162
Louis Martini Winery, 87
Mahoney Vineyards, 170
Marcassin Vineyard, 168
Martinelli Winery & Vineyards, 126
Matanzas Creek Winery, 127
Mayacamas Vineyards, 88

Merry Edwards Wines, 128
Chateau Montelena, 89
Morlet Family Vineyards, 90
Mount Eden Vineyards, 152
Newton Vineyard, 91
Nickel & Nickel, 92
Opus One, 93
Outpost Wines, 162
Pahlmeyer Winery, 94
Patz & Hall Wine Co., 129
Paul Hobbs Winery, 130
Peju Province Winery, 163
Peter Michael, 132
Philip Togni Vineyard, 95
Pine Ridge Winery, 163
Plumpjack, 163
Pride Mountain Vineyards, 96
Ramey Wine Cellars, 134
Ravenswood Winery, 168
Ridge Vineyards, 153
Ridge Vineyards (Lytton Springs), 135
Robert Biale Vineyards, 164
Robert Craig Wine Cellars, 164
Robert Foley, 97
Robert Mondavi Winery, 98
Rochioli Vineyards & Winery, 136
Rodney Strong Vineyards, 137
Saintsbury, 149
Sbragia Family Vineyards, 139
Schrader Cellars, 99
Screaming Eagle Winery, 100
Shafer Vineyards, 101
Silver Oak Cellars, 169
Robert Sinskey Vineyards, 102
Spottswoode Estate Vineyard & Winery, 103
St. Supéry Wines, 164
Stag's Leap Wine Cellars, 104
Staglin Family Vineyard, 105
Sterling Vineyards, 165
Stonestreet, 140
Tor Kenward Family Wines, 165
Trefethen Vineyards, 106
Turley Wine Cellars, 165
Turnbull Wine Cellars, 108
Vérité, 141
Viader Vineyards, 109
Vine Hill Ranch, 165
Vineyard 29, 110
Walter Hansel, 143
Whitehall Lane, 166
Williams Selyem, 144
ZD Wines, 111

Made in the USA
Columbia, SC
14 February 2019